Get Your Tenses Right

Get Your Tenses Right

Ronald Barnes

Drawings by David Bryant

Cambridge University Press
Cambridge
London · New York · Melbourne

Published by the Syndics of the Cambridge University Press
The Pitt Building, Trumpington Street, Cambridge CB2 IRP
Bentley House, 200 Euston Road, London NW1 2DB
32 East 57th Street, New York, NY 10022, USA
296 Beaconsfield Parade, Middle Park, Melbourne 3206,
Australia

© Cambridge University Press 1977

Library of Congress catalogue card number: 76–3040

ISBN 0 521 21296 0

First published 1977
Reprinted 1979

Set, printed and bound in Great Britain by
Cox & Wyman Ltd, London, Fakenham and Reading

Contents

Introduction

Many students of English have acquired a basic knowledge of English but still make mistakes in the tenses, especially when they speak. They have not had sufficient oral practice and are not clear about how the tenses should be used.

Most course books include a brief revision of the tenses with an explanation of their use and some written exercises. This book first systematically examines each tense separately with the emphasis on oral/aural practice, and then contrasts those tenses which cause most difficulty to students. An explanation of the use of the tenses as well as the tense changes in Reported Speech appear at the end of the book, which can be thus adapted to any method of teaching.

What the book contains
The book consists of 21 Units, a Summary of Tenses, a section on Reported Speech, and a list of Irregular Verbs.

Each Unit deals with one particular tense or compares the use of two or more tenses, e.g. Unit 4 Present Continuous, GOING TO, Simple Present. Each Unit is divided into five parts:

1 Presentation of the tense through a picture and dialogue.
2 Intonation exercise using the tense and other tenses previously introduced. Twenty of the basic English patterns are explained and practised.
3 Oral/Aural practice of the tense.
4 Listening comprehension. A dialogue based on the tense with questions for comprehension practice.
5 An exercise on the tense for written or oral work.

The Summary of Tenses at the end of the book explains the formation of each tense and its main uses. Although this is intended for the teacher, it may be useful to some students who like to study at home, especially if they were absent for a particular lesson.

A brief explanation of the tense changes from Direct to Indirect (Reported) Speech is also provided. Again this is for teachers, but it will also be useful to students for reference.

I

How to use the book

The following notes are intended as a guide to the teacher so that he may put the book to best use. An experienced teacher will naturally adopt the material to suit his or her own individual style of teaching and to meet the students' needs. Unit 9 is used as an example.

9.1 Presentation of the tense, in this case the Present Perfect. Books open. Discuss the picture first, then read the text. Explain any vocabulary and draw the students' attention to how the tense is used. Ask the questions and, where appropriate, relate them to the students, e.g. 'Have *you* just come back from France?' 'Have you ever been to France/ abroad?' 'Where have you been?'

9.2 Intonation. Books open. Demonstrate the pattern. Make the students aware of the different tunes by exaggerating the fall or rise of the voice. There may be resistance at first from students who think it is not important. Point out that their intonation is just as important as their English accent. ''What were your `holidays like?' and ''What were your ,holidays like?' have two different implications. The patterns can be revised later with books open or shut at the teacher's discretion.

9.3 Oral practice. Books shut. Elicit short and long answers by asking questions like this:

Teacher   Have you just had lunch?
Student   Yes, I have.
Teacher   What did he say?
2nd Student   He said he's just had lunch.

Where there is no sample dialogue, there is a prompt in the margin.

These questions should relate to actual classroom situations. Thus, if the question in the book is 'Have you just had lunch?', and the class is working in the morning, the question must obviously be changed to 'Have you just had breakfast?'

Ask these questions very fast, firing them at the students at random. Do only what is necessary: if they respond fluently and correctly, then stop before they become bored or restive. On the other hand, weak students can have further practice by forming the interrogative like this:

Teacher   Ask me if I've just had breakfast.

2

Student Have you just had breakfast?
Some Units have more than one type of Oral practice. These are marked a), b), c) etc., and correspond to the grammatical explanation of the Unit in the Summary of Tenses. e.g. 9.3 a) corresponds to the Summary of Tenses Unit 9 a).

9.4 Listening comprehension. Books shut. Set the 'scene' first by telling the students the names of the characters in the dialogue and where they are, e.g. 'Hugh is waiting at home for Wendy. She has just come back from the hairdresser's.'

Read the dialogue, or better, play the recording. Encourage the students to understand the general meaning of the dialogue first and not to lose track of the whole because of one word or phrase they do not understand. Read it again, then ask the questions on it.

Go over the dialogue with books open, explaining and commenting on the vocabulary and use of tense.

Both the dialogues in 9.1 and 9.4 can be used for pronunciation practice.

9.5 Writing. This can be done either in class or written for homework. Some Units have more than one exercise, marked a), b), c) etc. These correspond to the grammatical explanations of the Unit in the Summary of Tenses.

Some teachers may prefer to teach the change of tense in Reported Speech as they work through each Unit. The dialogues can be used as transformation exercises from Direct to Reported Speech.

Intonation
Before starting the book, explain the basic uses of the two tunes in English intonation.

Tune One The falling tune. The voice begins fairly high, and descends on each stressed syllable with the fall on the last main stressed syllable. The falling tune is used for
a) ordinary statements.
 I've just got back from France.
b) exclamations.
 Good heavens. What a pity.
c) questions beginning with question words
 (WHO/WHAT/WHERE/WHY/WHICH/WHEN/HOW?)

What time is it?
Where are you going?
How are you?

Tune Two The rising tune. Like the falling tune, the voice begins fairly high, descends on each stressed syllable but rises again on the last important word.
The rising tune is used for
a) ordinary questions.
   Are you going away on Saturday?
   Are you English?
   Is he coming?
b) sentences beginning with a subsidiary clause, followed by a main clause.
   The rising tune is usually used in the first part and the falling tune in the second.
   As soon as he got there, he felt ill.
c) sentences or questions with two objects.
   She speaks English and French.

Arrows have been used in the first 4 Units to demonstrate the rising and falling tunes. From Unit 5 the sign ` is used for the falling tune and ˌ for the rising tune, ' for high stress, and ˅for the fall–rise on one word, e.g. 'She's It`alian. ˅Spanish (`Spaˌnish). These signs are less obtrusive and easy to learn, so the student will be able to mark intonation in any book neatly and quickly. Only the main stress is marked in each case.

The recording
The dialogues and intonation practice are available on a recording.
   Play the first dialogue of each Unit while the student studies the picture. After discussion of the picture, play the recording again while the student follows the text.
   The second dialogue (4) of each Unit is a Listening comprehension. Play it twice with the student listening only before asking the questions. At the end of the questions, play it once with the books shut and again with the student following the text. Then make any necessary comments and explanations.
   Both the dialogue recordings can be used for pronunciation practice.
   The intonation practice should be played after the teacher

4

has demonstrated the pattern on the board. The student should
a) listen to the prompt
b) respond
c) listen to the correct response.

Reference
The following books are recommended for additional practice material and detailed explanation of intonation and stress:

Living English Speech, W. Stannard Allen (Longman)
Better English Pronunciation, J. D. O'Connor (Cambridge University Press)
Intonation of Colloquial English, J. D. O'Connor and G. F. Arnold (Longman)

For a more detailed explanation of the tenses:
A Practical English Grammar, A. J. Thomson and A. V. Martinet (Oxford University Press)

Unit 1

1.1 Reading

What's going on here?

Policeman	What's going on here?
Man	You mean, what's happening? Well, constable. I'm trying to get out of the window and Fred 'here is helping me.
Policeman	Why are you climbing through the window and not leaving by the front door?
Man	Well, you see I can't find the key and I'm in a hurry. Come on, Fred, we're wasting time.

Policeman	Just a minute you two. I don't think you're telling me the truth. This isn't your house, is it?
Man	No, it's my brother's. I'm staying with him for a while.
Policeman	Is he at home?
Man	I'm afraid not. He's in jail for house-breaking at the moment.

What's the man doing?
What's Fred doing?
What's the policeman doing?
Why aren't the men leaving by the front door?
Who's climbing through the window?
Who's the policeman talking to?
What's the man carrying?
Who's Fred looking at?
Who's the man staying with?

Do you think the man's telling the truth?
What do you think they're really doing?

1.2 Intonation

Tune One This isn't your house, is it?

The voice falls twice: once in the statement and once in the tag, with no pause between. This implies that you are sure of what you are saying and expect the other person to agree with you. It is *not* a question.
You're English, aren't you?
He isn't English, is he?

Now say these with the appropriate tags in the same way. There must be no hesitation between the statement and the tag. The comma is a formality and does not indicate a pause.
He's climbing out of the window, ... ?
Fred's helping him, ... ?
It isn't his house, ... ?
He's in a hurry, ... ?
He can't find the key, ... ?
He's not at home, ... ?
He's staying with his brother, ... ?
They're wasting time, ... ?
They aren't telling the truth, ... ?

7

We're working hard, ... ?
You're not concentrating, ... ?

1.3 Oral practice

Teacher	Are you listening to me?
Student	Yes, I am.
Teacher	What's he doing?
2nd Student	He's listening to you.

Are you/they listening to me/him/her?
Is he/she listening to me/them?
Am I sitting down/standing up/reading a book/going to the window/door/blackboard/teaching English/ learning English?
Is he/she sitting down, etc.?

What am I doing?
Where am I going?
What are you doing?
What are you wearing today?
What's she wearing?

1.4 Listening comprehension

Policeman stops a man and an old lady in the street.

Policeman	What's going on here?
Man	Nothing, constable. I'm helping this old lady across the street, that's all.
Policeman	Is that your suitcase?
Man	Er – as a matter of fact, it's the old lady's. I'm carrying it for her to the bus station.
Policeman	But the bus station is the other way.
Man	Oh, is it? Thank you for telling me. Anyway, I'm taking her to the bus station because she has to go to Brighton.
Policeman	But there aren't any buses to Brighton from here.
Man	Now you're confusing me, constable, and this poor old lady. Look, now she's crying.
Policeman	Excuse me, madam. What's the matter? Why are you crying?
Man	She can't understand you. She's a foreigner and can't speak English.

8

Policeman   Then how can you understand her?

Man   She's Russian, and I'm learning Russian at night-school. Goodbye, constable.

Is the man or the policeman helping the old lady across the street?

What's he carrying?

Whose case is it?

Where's he taking the old lady?

Why is he taking her to the bus station?

Is the old lady crying or laughing?

Why can't she understand the policeman?

Who's learning Russian?

Tune Two   *Ask me if*

he's helping her across the street.

he's taking her to the station.

she's crying.

he's learning Russian.

she can speak English.

Tune One   *Ask me*

where he's taking her.

what he's carrying.

why he's taking her to the bus station.

why she's crying.

what he's learning.

1.5 Writing

Put the verbs in brackets into the correct form: AM/ARE/IS DOING

1 She (sit) under the tree.

2 He's thirsty, so he (drink) a glass of water.

3 What you (do)? I (write) a letter.

4 We (look at) our books, but we not (read) them.

5 You not (study) German this year?

6 She not (speak) to me.

7 Where he (go)? He (go) home.

8 They (wait) for you outside.

9 They not (listen to) the radio.

10 Our teacher (stand up) but we (sit down).

Unit 2

2.1 Reading

How long are you going to stay in Paris?

Betty	George! What on earth are you doing here?
George	I'm booking a plane ticket to Paris.
Betty	When are you leaving?
George	Tomorrow afternoon.
Betty	Are you going on business or for pleasure?
George	On business. Our Paris representative is meeting me at the airport and taking me to the hotel. He's going to act as interpreter because I can't speak French very well.
Betty	How long are you going to stay in Paris?

George	Only a couple of days. My boss is arriving the day after tomorrow. We're going to have lunch together, and then we're going to talk to our Paris branch. Our firm isn't doing so well in France just now.
Betty	I'm sorry to hear that. By the way, what are you doing this evening?
George	I'm going to ring up Anne and ask her out to the pictures.
Betty	Oh. She's on holiday, isn't she?
George	No, not yet. She's going on holiday next week.
Betty	She's lucky. Well, have a good time in Paris.

Who's George talking to?
What's George doing at the travel agency?
When's he leaving for Paris?
Why's he going to Paris?
Who's meeting him at the airport?
Why is he going to act as interpreter?
How long is George going to stay in Paris?
When's his boss arriving?
What are they going to do after lunch?
Is George's firm doing well in France just now?
Who's George going to ring this evening?
When's Anne going on holiday?

2.2 Intonation

She's on holiday, isn't she? (I think she's on holiday, but I'm not sure. Do you know?)

Tune Two   When you are not sure of the answer and want the other person's opinion, your voice falls in the statement and rises in the tag. This is more like a question. Compare with Intonation 1.2.

He's coming, isn't he?
(I think he's coming, but I'm not sure.)
He isn't coming, is he?
(Is he coming? I don't really know.)

Now say these with the appropriate tags in the same way.
Remember no pause between statement and tag.
He's leaving for Paris, ... ?
He's going to stay for a couple of days, ... ?

He's going by air, ... ?
He isn't paying, ... ?
He can't speak French very well, ... ?
He's going to ring his girl-friend, ... ?
We're having dinner together, ... ?
You're not going, ... ?
They're going to have dinner together, ... ?
They're going to plan the following day's work, ... ?

2.3 Oral practice

Teacher	Are you going away this weekend?
Student	Yes, I am./No, I'm not.
Teacher	What did he say?
2nd Student	He said he's going away this weekend./He said he isn't going away this weekend.

Are you going away this weekend?
Are you coming to my lesson tomorrow/next week?
Are you meeting her after the lesson?
Are you playing football/basketball/tennis/golf/bridge this Saturday?
Are you leaving for New York tomorrow?
Are you having dinner with him tonight?
Are you going to work hard at your English?
Are you going to watch TV tonight?
Are you going to eat out tonight?

What are you going to do after the lesson?
What are you going to do this weekend?
Where are you going after the lesson?
Where are you going for Christmas/Easter/your summer holidays?

2.4 Listening comprehension

George on the phone to Anne

George	Hello. Is that you, Anne?
Anne	Yes, it is. Who's speaking?
George	This is George speaking. How are you?

Anne	Fine, thanks. How are *you*?
George	Not too bad. What are you doing?
Anne	Well, at the moment I'm watching television. There's a very good film on.
George	Oh, sorry to disturb you. I'm only ringing to ask you – what are you doing tonight?
Anne	I'm going to the theatre with my sister. She's coming here first for a meal.
George	Oh? What are you going to eat?
Anne	We're going to have an omelette. My sister's bringing some eggs and a bottle of red wine. We're going to eat about seven o'clock.
George	What are you going to see?
Anne	I'm not sure. She's buying the tickets. It's going to be a surprise.
George	Well, have a good time.
Anne	Thanks.
George	When am I going to see you again?
Anne	What about tomorrow? I'm not going out tomorrow.
George	I'm leaving for Paris in the afternoon. I'm going there on business for a couple of days.
Anne	Oh. See you next week then. Have a good trip.

What's Anne doing at the moment?
What's she doing tonight?
What are they going to eat?
What's Anne's sister bringing?
When are they going to eat?
When's George leaving for Paris?
Why's he going to Paris?
How long's he going for?

Who's speaking to Anne?
Who's coming for a meal?
Who's buying the theatre tickets?
Who's going to Paris?

Tune One *Ask me*
what Anne's doing at the moment.
what she's doing tonight.
who she's going with.
what they're going to eat.
what Anne's sister's bringing.

13

when George is leaving for Paris.
where he's going.
how long he's going for.

Tune Two   *Ask me if*
George is speaking to Anne on the phone.
she's going to the theatre tonight.
Anne's sister's coming for a meal.
they're going to have an omelette.
Anne's sister's buying the tickets.
Anne's going out tomorrow.
George's going to Paris on business.
he's going for a couple of days.

2.5 Writing

Put the verbs in brackets into the correct form: AM DOING/GOING
TO DO
(Some sentences can have both forms, depending on the
meaning.)

1   What you (do) this Sunday? I (play) golf.
2   What you (do)? We (watch) the telly.
3   I (have) an omelette for supper tonight.
4   They (see) me tomorrow.
5   Where they (go) for their summer holidays?
    They (go) to Japan.
6   Who he (write) to? He not (write) to anyone;
    he (write) a cheque.
7   My son (study) at university. He (be) an engineer.
8   What he (say)? He (speak) so quickly.
9   I not (go) out tonight.
10 I not (do) this again.

Unit 3

3.1 Reading

When in Rome . . .

Mr Turnbull   When in Rome, do as the Romans do, they say.
Mrs Turnbull   What *do* the Romans do?
Mr Turnbull   They live in Rome, of course, and go to work by car or bus.
               But sometimes it takes too long that way because of the traffic
               jams, so they walk.
Mrs Turnbull   In other words, the Romans do what everyone else does.
Mr Turnbull   Yes, but they do it differently. Everything is different.

15

Mrs Turnbull	What do you mean?
Mr Turnbull	Well, the climate's different for a start. It doesn't rain so much as it does in England. The sun shines more often.
Mrs Turnbull	I envy them the sun.
Mr Turnbull	I know. You hate the rain, don't you?
Mrs Turnbull	I certainly do.
Mr Turnbull	And a Roman really loves life. He knows how to enjoy himself.
Mrs Turnbull	They always eat spaghetti and drink wine, don't they?
Mr Turnbull	Not always. But they like a good meal. Lots of tourists go to Rome just for the food, you know.
Mrs Turnbull	Really? How much does it cost to fly to Rome?
Mr Turnbull	I don't know exactly, but it costs a lot of money.

Where do the Romans live?
How do they get to work?
Why do they sometimes walk?
What's different about the climate in Rome?
What does Mrs Turnbull envy?
What does she hate?
What does a Roman love?
Does he know how to enjoy himself?
Do the Romans always eat spaghetti and drink wine?
What do lots of tourists go to Rome for?
Does Mrs Turnbull know how much it costs to fly to Rome?

3.2 Intonation

Tune One The falling tune is used when you are sure of what you are saying.

I know you hate the rain = You hate the rain, don't you?

Tune Two The rising tune is used as an alternative to a question.

Don't they always eat spaghetti? = They always eat spaghetti, don't they?

Transform these in the same way. No pausing at commas.
I know they live in Rome.
I'm sure he loves life.
Don't they sometimes walk?
Don't you hate rain?
I'm sure he knows how to enjoy himself.

Do they always drink wine?
I'm sure you don't know.
I know they like a good meal.
I'm sure it doesn't rain so much.
Doesn't the sun shine more often?
Don't you live in Rome?

3.3 Oral practice

a)

Teacher	Where do you live?
Student	I live in Hamburg.
Teacher	What did he say?/Where does he live?
2nd Student	He said he lives in Hamburg./He lives in Hamburg.

Where do you/I live?
Where do the English/the French/the Greeks etc. live?
Where do you/they study English?
When do you/we have English lessons?
What do I teach?
When do I teach you English?
How often do you/they come here?
How do you/they get here?
How long do you take to get here?
How long does it take you to get here?
How long does it take to get to France/Germany etc. by car/train/air?
How much does it cost to fly to France etc?

b)

Tune One   *Ask me*
how many Italians I know.
how many Italians come to Britain every year.
how much money he earns.
how much of his money goes in taxes.
which language he speaks the best.
which student speaks the best English.
what we do next.
what happens next.
who they know in Rome.
who lives in Rome.

17

Mrs Smith meets Mrs Turnbull

Mrs Smith	Hello, Mrs Turnbull. How are you?
Mrs Turnbull	Fine, thanks. How's your boy, Jack?
Mrs Smith	He's a bit tired. You know, he goes to school at eight o'clock every morning. He doesn't get home till after four, then he does his homework after tea. It often takes him a couple of hours to finish it.
Mrs Turnbull	Poor boy. They work hard at school nowadays, don't they? Does he like it?
Mrs Smith	School, you mean? Yes, he does. He likes his teachers, and that always makes a difference.
Mrs Turnbull	Yes, it does. Does he go to school by bus?
Mrs Smith	No, he walks. He likes walking. He meets some of his friends at the corner and they go together.
Mrs Turnbull	What does he do when it rains?
Mrs Smith	My husband takes him in the car. He passes the school on the way to the office.

When does Jack go to school?
When does he get home?
When does he do his homework?
How long does it take him to do it?
Does he like school or does he hate it?
Does he like his teachers or does he hate them?
How does he get to school?
Where does he meet his friends?
How does he get to school when it rains?

Tune One	*Ask me*
	when Jack goes to school.
	when he gets home.
	when he does his homework.
	what he does after tea.
	how long it takes him to do it.
	where he meets his friends.
	how he gets to school when it rains.

Tune Two	*Ask me if*
	Jack goes to school at eight o'clock.
	he gets home after four.

he does his homework after tea.

it takes him a couple of hours to finish it.

they work hard at school nowadays.

he likes school.

he goes to school by bus.

he meets some of his friends at the corner.

they go to school together.

Mrs Smith's husband takes him to school when it rains.

3.5 Writing

Put the verbs in brackets into the correct form: DO/DOES

1 He never (go) to the theatre.
2 You (watch) television every night?
3 He always (pay) his bills promptly.
4 My father usually (shave) after breakfast.
5 How long it (take) to get to the office? It (take) me half an hour.
6 The Paris boat-train (leave) Victoria Station at 14.30.
7 You (know) how old I am?
8 Jane's husband not usually (smoke).
9 It not often (rain) in Egypt in August.
10 Florence (lie) on the River Arno.

Unit 4

4.1 Reading

The brush-off

George	Hello, Anne. What are you doing?
Anne	What I usually do at this time of night. I'm watching telly.
George	Do you always watch telly at this time?
Anne	Yes, I watch the news. I'm also smoking a cigarette and having a drink.
George	How many cigarettes do you smoke a day?
Anne	You're very nosey, aren't you? I smoke about fifteen. I think.

George	What are you drinking?
Anne	Heavens, you're worse than the Spanish Inquisition. I'm having a gin and tonic, if you must know. For your information, I usually have a gin and tonic and a cigarette when I watch the news, which I do every night at this time if I don't go out.
George	Actually, that's what I'm ringing you about. Are you going out tonight, by any chance?
Anne	No, I'm going to stay at home. Why?
George	Well, I'm going to the theatre and I've got a spare ticket, so—
Anne	That's very kind of you, George. But my sister's coming for a meal and—
George	Again?
Anne	What do you mean, again? She comes every week.
George	I'm beginning to think you don't want to see me.
Anne	What makes you say that?
George	You always give me the brush-off whenever I ask you out.

What's Anne doing?
Does she usually watch television at that time?
What else is she doing?
How many cigarettes does she smoke a day?
When does she usually have a drink and a cigarette?
What's Anne going to do tonight?
What's George going to do?
Who's coming for a meal?
Who comes every week?
Why does George think she doesn't want to see him?
Who gives him the brush-off whenever he asks her out?

4.2 Intonation

⌐She's watching television, but he isn't.

When you make a statement which contrasts two subjects, use the falling tune on the subject and the rising tune at the end of the phrase.

⌐She's watching television, but he isn't.

⌐He doesn't watch it every night, but she does.

Now say these in the same way, giving extra stress on the second subject. No pauses at commas.

She's smoking a cigarette, but he . . . . .
She smokes about fifteen a day, but he . . . . .
He's very nosey, but she . . . . .
He doesn't smoke, but she . . . . .
You're very good at this, but I . . . . .
You never make mistakes, but I . . . . .
He works hard, but they . . . . .
I'm going abroad this year, but they . . . . .
He doesn't want to go, but you . . . . .
They're going to eat when they get home, but you . . . . .
You don't understand him, but we . . . . .
He isn't tired, but we . . . . .

4.3   Oral practice

Revision

What did   Are you going to watch TV tonight?
he say?   Do you always watch TV at night?
Are you watching it now?

What are you going to do after the lesson?
Do you usually do that?
What are you doing now?

Are you going to have a cigarette after the lesson?
Do you usually have one after the lesson?
Are you smoking now?
How many cigarettes do you smoke a day?

When do you have English lessons?
Where do you have your English lessons?
Are you having one now?
How many lessons do you have a week?

Where do you come from?
Where are you living at the moment?
Are you going to live here permanently?

What are you going to do this weekend?
Where are you going after the lesson?
What do you usually do on Sundays?

Are you going to get up early tomorrow?
Do you get up early every morning?
When do you usually get up/go to bed?

Does he speak English well?
What language does he usually speak?
Is he speaking it at the moment?
Are you going to speak it after the lesson?

Tune One   *Ask me*
what I'm doing.
what I'm going to do after the lesson.
what I usually do on Sundays.
where I live.
where I'm living at the moment.
who he's speaking to.
who he speaks to every day.
who he's going to speak to this evening.
why I'm doing that.
why I always do that.
why I'm going to do that.

Tune Two   *Ask me if*
he lives in Edinburgh.
he's going to live in Edinburgh.
he's living in Edinburgh at the moment.
I'm working late tonight.
I'm going to work late tonight.
I work late every night.
she's working hard.
she works hard.
she's going to work hard.
I teach English.
I'm going to teach French as well.
I'm teaching English to foreigners.

4.4   Listening comprehension

Jim meets Peter on the way to the cinema

Peter   Hello, Jim. Where are you going?
Jim   To the cinema. What about coming with me?

Peter	No, thanks. I'm going home. My wife's expecting me.
Jim	What a pity. I believe it's a very good film.
Peter	Do you go to the cinema a lot?
Jim	Once a week. Most nights I sit at home and watch telly.
Peter	Do you know what's on tonight, by any chance?
Jim	No, I'm sorry I don't. I never read the papers till I get home.
Peter	Oh, I see. By the way, where are you going for your holidays this year?
Jim	I don't know yet. My wife's going to her mother's for a couple of weeks. She lives by the sea, you know.
Peter	Oh, does she? That's convenient.
Jim	Yes, but I want to go to the country.
Peter	Don't you like the sea?
Jim	Yes, very much. But I need peace and quiet when I'm on holiday. What are you going to do?
Peter	I'm going to stay at home.
Jim	Aren't you going to have a holiday abroad this year?
Peter	No. I want to buy a car, and that's going to take every penny I've got.

Where's Jim going?
How often does he go to the cinema?
Where's Peter going?
Why's he going home?
What does Jim do most nights?
When does he read the papers?
Where does Jim want to go for his holidays this year?
Where's Jim's wife going?
How long's she going for?
Where does her mother live?
Why does Jim want to go to the country?
What's Peter going to do for his holidays?
Why isn't he going abroad?

Who's going to the cinema?
Who goes to the cinema once a week?
Who's going to her mother's?
Who lives by the sea?
Who needs peace and quiet?
Who's going to stay at home?
Who wants to buy a car?

4.5 Writing

Put the verbs in brackets into the correct form: AM DOING/GOING
TO DO/DO
(Some sentences can have two forms, depending on the
meaning.)

1 I usually (clean) my teeth after every meal.
2 The Bournemouth train (leave) at 6.10.
3 He (learn) Spanish this year.
4 When you (do) your homework?
5 Her husband (write) articles for newspapers.
6 What you (do)? I (watch) telly.
7 We (play) tennis this afternoon. You never (ask) me to
play.
8 How many English people (live) in Madrid? I not (know).
9 How much it (cost) to go to Sicily by train?
10 They (think) they (know) everything.
11 My sister (take) her children to the swimming-pool
tomorrow.
12 Anyone (know) the answer to this question? No, no one
(know).
13 We (want) to go to the football match this afternoon.
14 How much money you (have)? Not much, I not (earn)
much where I (work).
15 When the film (begin)? It (begin) at 8.45.
16 My husband (ask) for more money at the end of the year.
17 Who (speak) on the phone? I not (know), because he
(speak) in Dutch and I not (understand) a word.
18 Which birds (make) their nests on the ground?
19 She (listen) to everything we (say). Then let's change the
subject.
20 I not (trust) her, because she (repeat) everything we (say)
to her friends.
21 You (know) where we (be)? I (think) so.
22 What this word (mean)?
23 Why she always (wear) such funny clothes? Because she
(have) no idea of fashion.
24 Who you (speak) to on the phone? I (speak) to George.
25 Look at that clear sky. It (be) a beautiful day.

Unit 5

5.1 Reading

What was the film like?

Peter	Hello, Jim. What was the film like?
Jim	Awful. It was a complete waste of time.
Peter	Why? What was it about?
Jim	It was about a married couple. They had to live with the wife's mother, because they didn't have enough money to buy a house of their own.
Peter	A lot of young people have to do that.
Jim	Yes, but the husband had to work overtime three times a

week, so he was always tired.

Peter	It sounds like the story of my life.
Jim	Yes, it does, doesn't it? But this man was always over-tired, and he couldn't sleep. So he used to take two sleeping pills every night.
Peter	I take sleeping pills sometimes.
Jim	Yes, but not two every night. Anyway, the strain was too much for him. He had a nervous breakdown and had to go to hospital.
Peter	It sounds a very depressing film.
Jim	Not really. His wife was able to find a good job as an interpreter, because she could speak French and German fluently. After a few months' work, she had a better job than her husband. So in the end, they were able to buy a house, and he didn't have to work any more. Stupid, wasn't it?
Peter	I don't know. My wife used to speak French. I must tell her to brush it up.

What was the film like?
What was a complete waste of time?
Why did the couple have to live with the wife's mother?
Why was the husband always tired?
Why did he use to take two sleeping pills every night?
Why did he have to go to hospital?
Why was his wife able to find a good job?
What were they able to do in the end?
Whose wife used to speak French well?

5.2 Intonation

It sounds like the story of your life.
Yes, it ˋdoes, ˋdoesn't it?

When you want to agree with someone politely, use the falling tune in both the statement and the tag. There are no pauses at the commas.

It wasn't a good film.
No, it ˋwasn't, ˋwas it?

Agree politely with the following:
It's cold today.

27

They aren't very friendly.
She speaks English well.
I don't like him.
He was rather rude.
I wasn't very nice to him.
He didn't have a car last year.
She had trouble getting here.
You didn't have to go.
They had to leave early.
He could speak English when he was a child.
I couldn't do it.
She was able to get here on time today.
I wasn't able to see him.
He used to live in Liverpool, you know.
He never used to do that.
There used to be a cinema at the end of the road.

5.3 Oral practice

a)
What was the weather like yesterday?
What was the date yesterday?
What day was it?
Where were you born?
Where was Shakespeare born?
When was the last time you were here?
How old were you when you started to learn English?

What did
he say?
Were you here yesterday?
Were you late for work this morning?
Were you hungry at breakfast time?
Were you born in London?
Was it cold yesterday?
Was Shakespeare English?
Was there a chair there at the last lesson?
Were there any desks in this room at the last lesson?

b)
When did you have breakfast?
What did you have for breakfast?
When did you have your last lesson?

28

Did you have breakfast this morning?
Did you have tea or coffee?
Did you have a good weekend?
Did you have good weather?
Did we have a lesson yesterday?
Did you have trouble getting here?
Did you have the same car last year?
Did you have a bicycle when you were a child?
Did you have a lot of money when you were young?

c)

Did you have to study Latin at school?
Did you have to get up early this morning?
Did you have to work late last night?
Did you have to do a lot of exams when you were at school?

When/where did you have to study Latin?
How much did you have to pay on the bus/tram/underground
this morning?
Who did you have to pay?

d)

What did
he say? Could you speak English when you were a child?
Could Shakespeare speak Russian?
Could you swim when you were a child?
Were you able to understand what I said just now?
Were you able to finish work early yesterday?
Were you able to get here on time today?

When were you first able to swim?
When were you first able to speak English/French/German etc.?
Which language could you speak first?
Which language could Shakespeare/Dante/Voltaire speak?

e)

What did
he say? Did you use to study Latin at school?
Did you use to go to school by bus?
Did you use to have difficulty in understanding English?
Did you use to live in Portugal?

When did you use to study Latin?
How did you use to get to school?
What did you use to study at school?

Where did you use to go on holiday when you were a child?

5.4 Listening comprehension

Betty and Jean on their way to work

Betty   What was the party like last night, Jean?

Jean   Not bad at all, thanks. There were one or two interesting people there. Why couldn't you come?

Betty   Well, I couldn't get away from work early. And when I got home I had a headache, so I had to go straight to bed. But I was over-tired, because I wasn't able to get to sleep for hours.

Jean   What a shame. Why didn't you take a sleeping pill?

Betty   I don't like them. I used to take them when I had to work overtime, you know.

Jean   How many did you use to take?

Betty   Three every night.

Jean   Good heavens. Why did you take so many?

Betty   Because I was under a terrible strain. The doctor said they weren't very strong. Anyway, I used to feel awful the next morning.

Jean   I'm sure you did.

Betty   The doctor said I had to be careful.

Jean   He was quite right.

Betty   So I stopped drinking coffee late at night instead.

What was the party like?
Why couldn't Betty go?
Why did she have to go straight to bed?
Why wasn't she able to get to sleep?
When did she use to take sleeping pills?
How many did she use to take?
Why did she take so many?
How did she use to feel the next morning?
What did the doctor say?

Who couldn't get away from work early?
Who was over-tired?
Who used to take sleeping pills?
Who was under a strain?
Who had to be careful?

Ask me if
it was a good party.
there were any interesting people there.
Betty had a headache.
she was tired.
she had to go straight to bed.
she was able to get to sleep immediately.
she used to take sleeping pills.
they were very strong.
she had to be careful.
she couldn't get away from work early.

Ask me
what the party was like.
why Betty couldn't go.
why she had to go straight to bed.
why she wasn't able to sleep.
how many sleeping pills she used to take.
who had to be careful.
who was right.

5.5 Writing

Put the correct forms into the blank spaces
1   . . . . . you at school yesterday?
2   It . . . . . hot last night.
3   We . . . . . a house by the sea last summer.
4   He . . . . . n't come last week because he . . . . . ill.
5   How old . . . . . you when you . . . . . first . . . .
    swim?
6   She . . . . . to play the piano very well when she . . . . .
    young.
7   . . . . . you have lunch early today?
8   . . . . . you . . . . get up early this morning?
9   Where . . . . . you born?
10 She . . . . leave the office early last night.

Unit 6

6.1 Reading

I enjoyed that very much

Pamela	That was good. I really enjoyed that. Thank you so much for asking me.
Bill	Not at all. Er – Pamela—
Pamela	Did you watch telly last night?
Bill	No, I didn't. I hardly ever watch television. Pamela—
Pamela	I did. I watched the football match. It was quite exciting.
Bill	Pamela—
Pamela	But it finished in a draw. Both teams played well, though.

32

	Actually, I tried to ring you, but you weren't in.
Bill	Did you?
Pamela	Yes. I wanted to tell you it was on.
Bill	Why?
Pamela	Because it was so exciting. All the fans shouted and clapped and cheered so much you could hardly hear the commentator. And I know how much you like football.
Bill	No, I don't. I hate it.
Pamela	Really? But you used to play it at school, didn't you?
Bill	Yes, I did. But I stopped playing years ago. Listen, Pamela—
Pamela	What's the matter? You look as white as a sheet. Is there anything wrong?
Bill	Yes, I'm afraid there is. I've got to tell you something.
Pamela	What?
Bill	I didn't bring any money with me. I can't pay the bill.

What did Pamela enjoy?
What did she watch on TV last night?
How did it finish?
Who played well?
Why did Pamela try to ring Bill?
Why could she hardly hear the commentator?
Did Bill use to play football at school?
When did he stop playing?
Why can't he pay the bill?

6.2 Intonation

I know you like football.
'No, I ˌdon't.
You don't like football.
'Yes, I ˌdo.

When you contradict or disagree with somebody, use the falling tune on the YES/NO and the rising tune on the auxiliary. The higher you start and finish the more indignant you sound. No pauses at commas.

Contradict or disagree with the following:
It's cold today.
They aren't very friendly.
You were rather rude to him.

I wasn't there at the time.
She used to have a lot of money.
You had a Rolls Royce last year.
He didn't like the film.
I tried to help you.
You couldn't do it.
You never worked hard.
The match finished in a draw.
Both teams played badly.

6.3 Oral practice

What did   Did you watch TV last night?
he say?   Did you enjoy it?
Did you learn French at school?
Did you like school?
Did you play tennis/golf/football yesterday?
Did he answer my last question?
Did he ask me a question?

What did you watch on TV last night?
When did you last watch TV?
When/where did you learn French?
What did you study at school?

6.4 Listening comprehension

Frank and Charles discuss last night's television programme

Frank   Did you watch television last night, Charles?
Charles   Yes, I did.
Frank   It was a good game, wasn't it?
Charles   Oh, I didn't watch the football match. I wanted to, but my wife preferred to look at the old film.
Frank   What a pity. It was quite exciting. Both teams played very well.
Charles   How did it finish?
Frank   It finished in a draw. What was the film like?
Charles   It was quite good. But I missed the beginning of it because I had to eat first.
Frank   Did your wife enjoy it?

34

Charles   No, she didn't. After half an hour she stopped watching and started to read a book.

What did Frank watch on television last night?
How did the match finish?
What did Charles watch on television last night?
Why didn't he watch the football match?
What was the film like?
Why did he miss the beginning of the film?
Did his wife enjoy the film?
What happened after half an hour?

Who watched the football match?
What was quite exciting?
Who missed the beginning of the film?
Who started to read a book?

Ask me if
he watched television last night.
he wanted to see the football match.
both teams played well.
the match finished in a draw.
he missed the beginning of the film.
his wife enjoyed it.
she started to read a book.

Ask me
what he watched on television last night.
why he didn't see the football match.
what he wanted to watch.
what his wife preferred to see.
how it finished.
why he missed the beginning.

who played well.
who enjoyed the film.
who missed the beginning.

6.5   Writing

Put the verbs in brackets into their Past form
1   I (answer) your letter by return of post.

35

2 My mother (die) at the age of ninety-two.
3 The new supermarket on the corner (open) two days ago.
4 Her new dress (fit) her perfectly when she (try) it on.
5 It (rain) the whole time I was on holiday.
6 The photographer's (develop) my film overnight.
7 He (hurry) down the street.
8 They (pray) for him to recover.
9 The baby (cry) all night.
10 The wet glass (slip) out of her hand and (drop) to the floor.

Unit 7

7.1 Reading

I understood most of what they said

Mrs Smith	Welcome home, Jack. Did you have a good journey?
Jack	Yes thanks, Mum. It was a bit rough crossing the Channel, but otherwise it was OK.
Mrs Smith	How did you get on with your French?
Jack	Not too badly. I understood most of what they said when they spoke slowly.
Mrs Smith	Were they nice to you?
Jack	Yes, very. They took me out in the car nearly every day.

	We went along the coast of Brittany. It took us three days there and back, because Pierre drove so slowly.
Mrs Smith	What was the food like?
Jack	I liked it. I ate everything they gave me, and drank wine with every meal.
Mrs Smith	Oh dear. I hope you didn't drink too much.
Jack	Of course I did. I got drunk every night and took drugs as well.
Mrs Smith	Jack! You are joking, aren't you!
Jack	What do you think?
Mrs Smith	Pierre seemed such a nice young man when I met him. I liked him very much.
Jack	So did I. I still do. I like his sister too.

What kind of journey did Jack have?
How did he get on with his French?
Where did they take him in the car?
Why did it take three days?
What did Jack eat?
How often did he drink wine?
What did Mrs Smith think of Pierre when she met him?

7.2 Intonation

I liked him very much.
'So did `I.
I didn't like him.
'Neither did `I.

This is a shorter way of saying:
I liked him very much too.
I didn't like him very much either.
Stress SO/NEITHER with the fall on the pronoun or noun.
No stress on the auxiliary.
He can swim.
'So can `she.
She doesn't speak French.
'Neither does her `brother.

Agree or disagree with the following:
He works hard. . . . . . I.

38

They're late.	. . . . . you.
I don't know.	. . . . . I.
He's going to do it.	. . . . . she.
He didn't enjoy the film.	. . . . . I.
I used to play tennis every day.	. . . . . I.
I had to learn Latin at school.	. . . . . I.
They enjoyed themselves.	. . . . . we.
I didn't understand what she said.	. . . . . he.
They weren't there.	. . . . . I.
He couldn't do it.	. . . . . you.
She was hungry.	. . . . . Bill.
They went home early.	. . ./. . she.
He saw the film yesterday.	. . . . . Pamela.

7.3   Oral practice

What did
he say?

Did I see you in the street this afternoon?
Did I speak to you just now?
Did Shakespeare write Hamlet?
Did you know any English last year?
Did you know me last year?
Did you come to school yesterday?
Did you go abroad for your holidays last year?
Did you go to the football match last week?
Did you go with him?
Did you understand what I said?
Did you do your homework last night?
Did you read the paper this morning?
Did you hear the news on the radio this morning?
Did you sit there last time?
Did you feel tired after work last night?
Did you put your car away last night?
Did you leave your car in the street last night?
Did it take you a long time to get here this morning?
Did you bring any money with you today?
Did you think of going away for the weekend?
Did I teach you last year?
Did you eat a lot for lunch today?
Did you drink any wine with it?

What did you eat for lunch?
Where did you eat it?

When did you leave home this morning?
Where did you buy that book?
Where did you get that tie?
Where did you leave your car?
How did you get here?
How long did it take you to get here?
How much did it cost?
What did you do after the last lesson?
Where did you think of going after the lesson?
What did you do last Sunday?

Extra oral practice

Make the following sentences interrogative:

He gave her a present.	They went all the way home.
sent	came
brought	drove
bought	stood
got	sat
made	read
took	spoke
	felt ill

I met them yesterday.	He ate everything.
saw	drank
taught	said
left	understood
thought of	lost
wrote to	won
	heard
	did
	sold
	put down
It cost a lot.	knew

7.4 Listening comprehension

Bill and Harry talk about what they did last night

Bill   Hello, Harry. Where were you last night? I looked for you everywhere.

40

Harry	I went to Pamela's. She gave a party for some American friends of hers.
Bill	Did you enjoy yourself?
Harry	Very much indeed, thanks. I met a lot of interesting people. Why didn't you come?
Bill	She didn't ask me.
Harry	How funny. I thought she liked you.
Bill	She used to. But not now.
Harry	Why not?
Bill	Because I asked her out to dinner a month ago.
Harry	Didn't she want to go?
Bill	Oh yes, she wanted to go all right. We went to that new restaurant in the High Street. She ate for two hours without stopping.
Harry	She liked the food then?
Bill	Oh yes. She liked the food all right.
Harry	Then what happened? What went wrong?
Bill	I forgot to take any money with me.
Harry	Good heavens. So what did you do?
Bill	I phoned home, and eventually my brother brought some money to the restaurant. But it took him an hour to get there.
Harry	Why did it take him so long?
Bill	I think he wanted to teach me a lesson.

Where did Harry go last night?
Who did Pamela give the party for?
What kind of people did Harry meet?
Why didn't Bill go?
When did he ask Pamela out to dinner?
Did she want to go?
Where did they go?
How long did she eat for?
Did she like the food?
What went wrong?
Where did Bill phone?
How long did it take his brother to get to the restaurant?
Why did it take him so long?
Who gave the party last night?
Who asked Pamela out to dinner a month ago?
Who forgot to take any money?
Who brought Bill the money?

Ask me if
Harry went to Pamela's last night.
she gave a party.
he met a lot of interesting people.
Bill went.
Pamela ate a lot.
Bill forgot to take any money.
his brother brought the money.
it took him an hour to get there.

Ask me
where Harry went last night.
who Pamela gave the party for.
who he met.
where they went for dinner.
how much she ate.
who forgot to take any money.
what he did.
who brought the money.
how long it took him to get there.

7.5 Writing

Put the verbs in brackets into their Past form
1 He (send) his luggage in advance.
2 We (drive) to Leicester from Birmingham and (get) there
   in under two hours.
3 My sister (see) you in the street this afternoon.
4 I (drink) a litre of wine at the party and (eat) a cheese
   sandwich.
5 You (put) your cheque in the bank this morning? No, I
   (put) it in yesterday.
6 He (meet) her for the first time last week and immediately
   (make) a date to see her again.
7 She (give) her mother-in-law a bracelet for Christmas.
8 We (read) the last lesson in class.
9 My wife's fur coat (cost) a lot of money.
10 The teacher (speak) to her in English and she (understand)
    everything he (say).
11 Who (write) Hamlet?
12 He (think) he (know) her.
13 When they (lose) their money, they (sell) their house.

42

14 When they (win) the Pools, they (buy) a big house.
15 He (take) me to the concert and we (hear) some Chopin.
16 I (work) hard yesterday and (do) a lot of things.
17 I (leave) the party early because Allan (bring) me home.
18 I (feel) tired when I (come) home so I (go) straight to bed.
19 My wife (sit) in the bus but I (stand).
20 Who (teach) you last year?

Unit 8

8.1 Reading

What were you doing last night?

Anne	George. What on earth are you doing here?
George	I was looking for you.
Anne	You know my boss doesn't like you coming here during office hours. What do you want?
George	What were you doing last night when I rang you?
Anne	What time did you ring me?
George	About seven. I told you I was going to ring you.
Anne	So you did. Are you sure you dialled the right number?

44

George	Of course I am. I tried three times, and in the end I got so fed up that I asked the operator to try. She said your phone was out of order.
Anne	Oh, now I remember. I left the receiver off the hook. I was writing some letters and I didn't want to be disturbed. What did you want anyway?
George	Nothing in particular. I was going to ask you to the pictures, that's all.
Anne	Oh, I see. As a matter of fact, I was working hard.
George	I thought you said you were writing letters.
Anne	So I was. I find that very hard work.

What was George doing in Anne's office?
What did he want to know?
When did he ring Anne last night?
How many times did he try to ring her?
What did he do in the end?
What was Anne doing when George rang?
Where was George going to ask her that evening?
What did Anne say she was doing?

8.2 Intonation

I told you I was going to ring you.
So you ˅did.
It's raining.
So it ˅is.

This is another way of saying: That's true. You're right. You show surprise, either because you have forgotten or because you have not noticed something.
so is unstressed and the high fall is on the auxiliary.

Show surprise at the following:
They were going to the cinema.
We were going to ring them this morning.
He's living in Madrid now.
It's snowing.
Shakespeare said that.
We can see them tomorrow.
You said you had to work late.
There used to be a cinema there once.

45

They used to live next door.
I was right.
She was able to find it by herself.
I did it myself.

8.3 Oral practice

What did Were you studying English a year ago?
he say? Were you working for the same firm last year?
Were you living in the same house last year?
Were you smoking a cigarette when I came in?
Were you wearing that sweater/dress yesterday?
Was it raining/snowing when you came here?
Were you talking to her when I came in?
Was she talking to you just now?
When was she talking to you?
What were you wearing yesterday?
Who were you working for last year?
Where were you living last year?
Where were you studying English last year?
What were you doing when I came into class?
What were you doing at this time yesterday?
What were you doing at eight o'clock last night?

8.4 Listening comprehension

George on the phone again to Anne

George Is that you, Anne?
Anne Yes, it is. That's George, I suppose.
George Yes. Listen, where were you going when I saw you in the street this afternoon?
Anne I was going home. Why?
George Well, you were walking so fast I thought you had another date.
Anne Well, I didn't.
George I tried to ring you up later, but the number was always engaged.
Anne I expect it was.
George What were you doing?
Anne As a matter of fact, I was talking to my sister.

46

George	But I rang three times. I got so fed up that in the end I asked the operator to try.
Anne	I left the receiver off the hook.
George	Why?
Anne	Because I was working and I didn't want to be disturbed.
George	What kind of work were you doing?
Anne	If you must know, I was checking some figures for my boss.
George	Why didn't you ask me to help? You know I'm good at figures.
Anne	Because it was secret and confidential.
George	Oh, sorry. I was only trying to help.

Where was Anne going when George saw her in the street?
Why did he think she had another date?
What was Anne doing when George tried to ring her?
Why did he ask the operator to try in the end?
Why did Anne leave the receiver off the hook?
What kind of work was she doing?
Why didn't she ask George to help her?

Who saw Anne in the street?
Who was walking fast?
Who tried to ring her later?
Who was talking to her sister?
What was always engaged?
Who's good at figures?

Ask me if
she was going home.
she was walking fast.
she was talking to her sister.
George rang three times.
she was working.
she didn't want to be disturbed.
she was checking some figures for her boss.
George is good at figures.
he was trying to help.

Ask me
where she was going.
why he thought she had another date.
what she was doing.

47

who she was talking to.
who she was working for.

8.5 Writing

a) *Put the verbs in brackets into the correct form:* DID/WAS DOING
1 I (have) breakfast when the post (come).
2 He (grow) a beard the last time I (see) him.
3 They (pay) the bill as they (leave).
4 It not (rain) heavily, so we (go) for a walk.
5 He (fall) asleep while he (drive).
6 What you (do) when I (ring) you?
7 He (tell) us he (go) to Mexico for his holidays.
8 You (talk) to her when I (arrive)?
9 You (work) for the same firm last year as you are now?
10 She not (wear) that dress when we (meet).

b) *Put the verbs in brackets into the correct form:* WAS DOING/
USED TO DO
1 When I was rich, I (buy) a lot of clothes.
2 He (talk) to someone just now.
3 I always (read) under the bedclothes when I was young.
4 I broke my leg while I (ski).
5 What you (do) at eight o'clock last night?
6 I (be) good at maths when I was at school.
7 My daughter (practise) the piano every day, but now she
doesn't play at all.
8 It (snow) when we went out.
9 We (be) good friends at university, but now we hardly
ever see each other.
10 George only (try) to help Anne.

Unit 9

9.1 Reading

I've just got back from France

Richard   What were your holidays like?

Jack   Super. I went to France.

Richard   Did you?

Jack   Yes. I've just got back. I came back yesterday, as a matter of fact.

Richard   Aren't you lucky. I've never been abroad.

Jack   Oh, I've been to France twice. We've got friends there.

Richard   How long were you there for?

49

Jack	I stayed nearly a fortnight.
Richard	Did you speak French all the time?
Jack	Most of the time. I think my French has improved a lot.
Richard	What does old Thompson think?
Jack	Our French teacher? I haven't seen him yet.
Richard	I saw him in the corridor a couple of minutes ago. His lesson has already started. We're late.
Jack	Oh well, it's our first day back, and I've never been late before. Did you have a good time?
Richard	I stayed at home. The weather's been awful here. I think this is the worst spring we've ever had. As a matter of fact, this is the first day we've had any sun. And now we're back at school.

Where did Jack go for his holiday?
Has he just got back?
When did he get back?
Has Richard ever been abroad?
How many times has Jack been to France?
How long was he there for this time?
What does Jack think about his French?
Has he seen Thompson yet?
Where did Richard see him?
What's already started?
Has Jack ever been late before?
What's the weather been like?
What does Richard think about the spring?

9.2 Intonation

'What were your ‚holidays like?

So far, questions beginning with question words like WHO/
WHAT/WHY/HOW/WHEN have had the falling tune:
'What were your ˋholidays like?

But when you want to show a particular interest, use the
rising tune as in a normal question.
'Did you en'joy your ‚holidays?
'What were your ‚holidays like?

Ask the following questions and show that you are really

interested to know the reply:

Where's your mother?
Where have you been?
Which one do you want?
Why didn't you ring me last night?
How's your grand-daughter?
How long have you been married?
Where did you go for your holiday this year?
How many times have you been to Greece?
What did you think of it?
When did you get back?
How many children have you got?
How much do you want for your car?
Who were you talking to just now?

9.3 Oral practice

a)

What did he say?

Have you just arrived?
Have you just had lunch?
Have you already had breakfast?
Have you done the First Certificate examination yet?
Have you been to the States yet?
Is this the first time you've done this exercise?
Have you just come in/or gone out?
Has he just answered a question or asked one?
Have you just had breakfast or lunch?

b)

Have you already had lunch?
When/where did you have it?
What did you have?
Have you just answered a question?
When did you last answer a question?
Have you seen me before?
When was the last time you saw me?
How often have you seen me this week?
When did you see me?
Have you ever been abroad?
Where have you been?
When did you go there?
Did you like it?

51

Have you ever read a book in English?
What was it called?
When did you read it?
Have you had a cigarette today?
Have you just finished one?
How many have you smoked today?
Have you just come in?
When did you come in?
Is this the first time you've been here?
Have you been here before?
When was the last time you were here?
Have you watched TV lately?
Did you watch TV last night?
What did you see?
When was the last time you watched TV?
Have you seen any good films lately?
What did you see?
Where did you see it?

9.4 Listening comprehension

Hugh waiting at home for Wendy

Hugh	You're late home, Wendy. Where have you been?
Wendy	I've been to the hairdresser's.
Hugh	The hairdresser's? Haven't you already been there this week?
Wendy	Yes, I have. I went last Tuesday. But I didn't like the way he did it. As a matter of fact, this is the first time he's done it nicely.
Hugh	It looks the same to me.
Wendy	That's a typical man's remark. Have you had tea yet?
Hugh	No. I was waiting for you.
Wendy	Well, we haven't got much time, you know. Have you forgotten we're going to the cinema?
Hugh	The cinema? This is the first I've heard of it.
Wendy	Hugh, I told you this morning. I mean, I asked you, and you promised to take me.
Hugh	What's on anyway?
Wendy	'The Scotsman in Brussels'.
Hugh	I've already seen it.
Wendy	When did you see it?
Hugh	I saw it last week. I went with Jim.

Wendy	You never told me you went to the cinema with Jim last week.
Hugh	Do I have to tell you everything?
Wendy	Yes, of course you do. We're married, aren't we? Anyway, I haven't seen it and I'm going tonight even if I have to go by myself.
Hugh	I hope you enjoy it. I thought it was awful.

Where's Wendy been?
Has she already been there this week?
When did she go?
Why has she been again?
Why hasn't Hugh had tea yet?
Has Hugh forgotten they are going to the cinema?
When did Wendy ask him to take her to the cinema?
What's on at the cinema?
When did Hugh see the film?

Who did he go with?
Who's Wendy married to?
Has Wendy seen the film?
When's she going to see it?
What did Hugh think of the film?

Ask me if
she's been to the hairdresser's.
she's already been there this week.
Hugh's had tea yet.
he's forgotten they were going to the cinema.
he's already seen the film.
he went last week.
Wendy's seen the film.

Ask me
where Wendy's been.
why Hugh hasn't had tea yet.
why they haven't got much time.
when Hugh saw the film.
who he went with.
who Wendy's married to.

9.5 Writing

a)

Put the verbs in brackets into the correct form: HAVE DONE

1 You already (do) your homework?
2 I not (finish) that book yet.
3 I not (see) him recently.
4 She just (buy) that dress.
5 You just (have) lunch?
6 They already (leave).
7 This is the second time I (tell) you to learn this.
8 You (read) any good books lately?
9 He's the nicest person I ever (meet).
10 This is the first time you (be) in this room?

b)

Put the verbs in brackets into the correct form: DID/HAVE DONE

1 I (buy) that dress two months ago, but I not (wear) it yet.
2 My wife just (have) a baby.
3 Is this the first time you (be) to England?
4 You (see) my brother? Yes, he just (come in).
5 When you (arrive)? I (arrive) a minute ago.
6 I (decide) to live here permanently.
7 I not (see) your sister on the bus today.
8 I not (see) your sister today.
9 I not (see) your sister this morning. No, she (go) to the country for the weekend.
10 You (be) to New York? No, but my brother (go) there last year.
11 This is the first day we (have) any sun.
12 He always (be) a good student in this class.
13 He always (be) a good student when he was here.
14 They (leave) for London yet?
15 Where you (buy) that hat? I (get) it at a sale.
16 You're late. Where you (be)? I (be) to the hairdresser's.
17 How much your new bag (cost)?
18 You (read) Hamlet? Yes, as a matter of fact I (read) it last night.
19 You (have) lunch yet? Yes, thanks. I already (eat).
20 I (lose) my watch. Where you (lose) it? I (lose) it in the street.

Unit 10

10.1 Reading

What have you been doing?

Mr Turnbull	Oh, there you are. I've been waiting for you for half an hour. What have you been doing?
Mrs Turnbull	I've been shopping. I've bought a new hat. Do you like it?
Mr Turnbull	It's all right. I met the Smiths' son, Jack, while I was waiting for you. He's just come back from France.
Mrs Turnbull	Yes, I know. Mrs Smith told me. She's very proud of him. She says he speaks French fluently.
Mr Turnbull	How long has he been learning it?
Mrs Turnbull	I'm not sure.

55

Mr Turnbull	What did you say?
Mrs Turnbull	I said I'm not sure. I think he's been studying French since he was twelve.
Mr Turnbull	Who's been studying French?
Mrs Turnbull	Jack has. The Smiths' son. Have you gone deaf or something?
Mr Turnbull	I can't hear a word you're saying. The noise of this traffic is absolutely awful.
Mrs Turnbull	Yes, it is, isn't it? Goodness, I'm tired. I've been walking round the shops for nearly three hours.
Mr Turnbull	(*misunderstanding her*) Three hours? What do you mean? I've been working since eight o'clock this morning.

How long has Mr Turnbull been waiting for his wife?
What has she been doing?
What's she bought?
When did he meet Jack?
Where's Jack been?
Who's been studying French?
Why can't Mr Turnbull hear what his wife is saying?
Why is Mrs Turnbull tired?
How long has Mr Turnbull been working?

10.2   Intonation

He's been studying French.
,Who's been studying French? (,What did you say?)

When you want the other person to repeat what he has just said, use the rising tune with the stress on the question word.
   Begin low and continue to rise with no main stress on the other words.

Where did you see him?
,Where did I see him? (Did you say Where? or When?)

This pattern often shows surprise.

Why are you studying French?
,Why? (Because I want to, of course.)

Ask the other person to repeat what he has said or asked in the same way:

56

She lives in Mousehole.	Where	.....?
His name is Cholmondeley.	What	.....?
Arrigo Panigada won the championship.	Who	.....?
We went to Beaulieu.	Where	.....?
Why do you smoke so much?	Why	.....?
I've been studying Chinese for twenty years.	What	.....?
It's been raining for two weeks.	How long	.....?
They've bought Waterloo Bridge.	What	.....?
Why did you go to the concert?	Why	.....?
We went ski-ing last August.	When	.....?
He bought Jim's old car.	Whose	.....?
They were travelling on a cattle boat.	What	.....?

10.3 Oral practice

What did
he say?

How long have you been studying English?
How long have you been living here/working at your job/
smoking/driving a car?
How long have I been teaching you?
What have I been teaching you?
What have you been doing for the past half hour?
What have you been studying recently?
Have you been working hard today?

Ask me if
I've been working hard today/living here for many years/
teaching English for many years.

Ask me
how long I've been teaching English/living here.
how long he's been learning English/living here.
what I've been doing today/he's been studying recently.
where I've been living/he's been working/she's been living.
which firm he's been working for.

10.4 Listening comprehension

Jean waiting for Betty

Betty Sorry I'm late, Jean. Have you been waiting for me?
Jean Of course I have. I've been waiting for nearly half an hour.

We arranged to meet at three, and it's almost half past.
What have you been doing all this time?

Betty   I've been looking for a flat.

Jean   A flat?

Betty   Yes, somewhere to live. My landlady's daughter is getting married and wants to move into my flat.

Jean   What a shame. How long have you been living there?

Betty   Three years or so. But it's really too big for me, and I've been looking for something smaller for the last six months.

Jean   Have you had any luck yet?

Betty   Yes, I think so. I've just seen a very nice one. But it's very dirty: an old couple have been living there for the last thirty years.

Jean   How much is the rent?

Betty   I'm not sure. I've got to ring the agents after six this evening.

Jean   I hope you get it, Betty.

Betty   So do I. Other people have been looking at the flat, so I must be sure to ring at six o'clock on the dot.

How long has Jean been waiting for Betty?
When did they arrange to meet?
What's Betty been doing?
Why has she been looking for a flat?
How long has she been living there?
How long has she been looking for something smaller?
What has she just seen?
How long have the old couple been living in the flat?
What's the matter with the flat?
Why must she be sure to ring the agents at six o'clock?

Ask me if
Jean's been waiting for Betty.
she's been looking for a flat.
she's been living in her flat for three years.
she's been looking for something smaller.
she's had any luck yet.
she's just seen a nice one.
an old couple have been living there.
other people have been looking at it.

Ask me
how long she's been waiting for Betty.
what Betty's been doing.

58

how long she's been living there.
how long she's been looking for something smaller.
how long the old couple have been living there.
what she's just seen.

10.5   Writing

Put the verbs in brackets into the correct form: HAVE BEEN DOING
and SINCE *or* FOR *into the blank spaces*
1   I (live) in Switzerland . . . . . two and a half years.
2   My father (work) for that firm . . . . . 1964.
3   She (play) the piano . . . . . she was a child.
4   He (write) that book . . . . . eighteen months.
5   They (paint) their house . . . . last week.
6   How long you (study) English? I (study) English . . . . .
    a year.
7   You (talk) to your friend . . . . . I came in.
8   It (rain) . . . . . breakfast.
9   What he (do) . . . . . the past hour?
10 Our teacher says he (teach) English . . . . . he was twenty.

Unit 11

11.1 Reading

After he had gone, I began to worry about him

Mrs Smith	Hello, Mrs Turnbull. Fancy meeting you here. I haven't seen you for a long time.
Mrs Turnbull	No, we haven't met since your boy Jack came back from France.
Mrs Smith	No, that was a month ago. He has been talking of nothing else since then.
Mrs Turnbull	It was the first time he had been abroad, wasn't it?

Mrs Smith	No, the second.
Mrs Turnbull	Did you go with him?
Mrs Smith	No, I wish I had. Because after he had gone, I began to worry about him. He's only sixteen, you know. And since he came back, he's been talking about living there.
Mrs Turnbull	I know what you mean. My daughter's the same.
Mrs Smith	Oh yes, the last time I saw you, you said you'd been to Scotland for the weekend.
Mrs Turnbull	That's right. I went to see her and my son-in-law. They had just come back from Canada.
Mrs Smith	How long had they been there?
Mrs Turnbull	Actually, they wanted to stay for good. But they hadn't been there for long when they began to feel homesick.
Mrs Smith	So now they've come back to Scotland, have they?
Mrs Turnbull	For the moment. They keep moving about from one place to another. They used to be next door to us, but they hadn't been living there for long before they moved to Scotland. Then to Canada. Now back to Scotland again. They're restless, these young people.

How long is it since Mrs Smith saw Mrs Turnbull?
Was it the first time Jack had been abroad?
Why did Mrs Smith wish she had gone with him?
What's Jack been talking about since he came back from France?
Why had Mrs Turnbull been to Scotland?
Where had her daughter and son-in-law come back from?
How long had they been in Canada?

11.2 Intonation

Did you go with him?
No, I 'wish I ˋhad (gone with him).

When you wish you had or had not done something in the past at the moment of speaking, say: I 'wish I ˋHAD./I 'wish I ˋHADN'T.

You smoke a lot, don't you?
Yes, I 'wish I ˋdidn't (smoke a lot). (I'm sorry I smoke a lot.)
When you wish for or want something at the moment of speaking, but which is not true, say:

I wish + subject + auxiliary of Past tense.
Stress WISH with the falling tune on the auxiliary.

Wish the following:
Did you go to Pamela's party?	No, I wish I . . . . .
Did you buy that new dress you wanted?	No, I wish I . . . . .
You speak German, don't you?	No, I wish I . . . . .
Is your daughter good at languages?	No, I wish she . . . . .
You've got a lot of money, haven't you?	No, I wish I . . . . .
Your husband earns a lot, doesn't he?	No, I wish he . . . . .
They're coming to see us this afternoon, aren't they?	Yes, I wish they . . . . .
Do you have to go now?	Yes, I wish I . . . . .
Have you been to South America?	No, I wish I . . . . .
You're very clever, aren't you?	No, I wish I . . . . .
Did you spend a lot of money in that shop?	Yes, and I wish I . . . . .
You're married, aren't you?	Yes, and I wish I . . . . .

11.3   Oral practice

Teacher   Have you been studying English/FOR LONG?
                                                    /FOR A LONG TIME?

Student   Yes, I have./No, I haven't.
Teacher   How long has he been studying English?
2nd Student   *He's been studying* English FOR A LONG TIME.
              He hasn't been studying English FOR LONG.

Have you been studying English for long/for a long time?
Have you been living here for long/for a long time?
Have you been working at your job for long/for a long time?
Have you been driving a car for long/for a long time?
Have you been smoking for long/for a long time?
Have you been playing tennis/the piano/the guitar for long/
for a long time?

Teacher   How long is it since we saw each other?
Student   *We haven't seen* each other FOR A LONG TIME./*We saw* each
              other yesterday.
Teacher   What did he say?

62

| 2nd Student | He said *you hadn't seen* each other FOR A LONG TIME./He said *you saw* each other yesterday. |

How long is it since/we saw each other?
/you had a holiday?
/you went to the cinema?
/you smoked your last cigarette?
/I saw you?
/we had any homework?
/you went home to your parents?
/I asked you a question?

How long have you been/studying English?
/living here?
/working at your job?
/driving a car?
/smoking?
/playing tennis/the piano?

11.4 Listening comprehension

Harry meets Bill

Harry   Hello, Bill. I haven't seen you for a long time. What have you been doing?
Bill   I've been working hard as usual. And you?
Harry   I've been on holiday.
Bill   Aren't you lucky. Where did you go?
Harry   I went to Spain. I'd never been there before.
Bill   Did you have a good time?
Harry   Marvellous, thanks. Guess who I met on the plane coming back.
Bill   Who?
Harry   Pamela.
Bill   Pamela? Pamela Carter, you mean. How is she?
Harry   Fine. She was asking about you. She said she hadn't seen you for nearly three months.
Bill   I know. We haven't seen each other since I took her to that restaurant in the High Street. Remember?
Harry   Yes, I do. You forgot to take any money. Anyway, I think she's forgiven you. Why don't you give her a ring and ask her out to dinner?

Bill	If you're sure she's forgotten that ghastly evening.
Harry	I didn't say she had forgotten it. I said she had forgiven you. So ring her up at once. You've got her number, haven't you?
Bill	Er – I think so. But I've lost her address.
Harry	You're the most absent-minded man I know. Well, I'm not going to do any more for you. You can ask her for her address yourself. And one more thing.
Bill	What's that?
Harry	Remember to take some money with you this time.

How long is it since Harry saw Bill?
What's Bill been doing?
Where's Harry been?
Had he been to Spain before?
Who did Harry meet on the plane coming back?
How long did Pamela say it was since she had seen Bill?
Did Harry say Pamela had forgotten that evening?
What *did* he say?
What's Bill lost?
What must Bill remember to take next time?

Who's been working hard?
Who hadn't been to Spain before?
Who was asking for Bill on the plane?
Who hadn't seen Bill for three months?

Ask me if
Bill's been working hard.
Harry's been on holiday.
he went to Spain.
he'd never been there before.
Pamela was asking about Bill.
she hadn't seen him for nearly three months.
she's forgiven Bill.

Ask me
what Bill's been doing.
where Harry's been.
when he had been there before.
how long it is since Pamela saw Bill.
what Bill's forgotten.

64

11.5 Writing

a)

Put the verbs in brackets into the correct form: HAD DONE/HAD
BEEN DOING

1 He didn't come to the film with us yesterday, because he already (see) it.
2 After she (eat) her supper, she went to bed.
3 It was the second time I (read) the novel.
4 We (travel) for two hours before we realized we were on the wrong train.
5 As soon as he (do) his homework, the boy ran into the garden.
6 He said he (work) hard all day.
7 The children (play) outside for an hour when it began to rain.
8 She only just (leave) the house when her husband phoned.
9 He told me he was tired because he (drive) since eight o'clock this morning.
10 Was it the first time you ever (be) there?

b)

Put the verbs in brackets into the correct form

1 I not (play) tennis for a long time.
2 I not (play) tennis for long.
3 We not (dance) for a long time, have we?
4 I not (work) for that firm for long.
5 I not (teach) for long
6 They not (live) there for long, before they moved to Scotland.
7 He made a lot of mistakes, because he not (speak) French for a long time.
8 He not (drive) for long when he came to the cross-roads.
9 He not (walk) for long when he saw the river.
10 He was very depressed because he not (work) for a long time.

c)

Put the verbs in brackets into the correct form

1 She not (drive) for long.
2 He not (do) any homework for a long time.
3 It not (rain) for long.
4 She not (swim) for long before she began to feel cold.

5   This is the first time he (go) to England for many years. Actually, he not (be) since the war.
6   They not (see) each other for a long time.
7   I wanted to go to the theatre because I not (be) for a long time.
8   My brother not (live) in Manchester for long before he had to move to Birmingham.
9   I wrote him a long letter because I not (hear) from him for a long time.
10   She not (read) for long before she fell asleep.
11   I (have) this cold for two weeks.
12   How long you (be) here? I (be) here for an hour.
13   We not (be) to the pictures for a long time. As a matter of fact, I don't think I (be) since my last birthday.
14   How long you (wait)?
15   Our teacher told us he (teach) English since he was twenty.
16   He not (have) his new car for long before he had an accident.
17   You (be) on holiday? Yes, I (be) to Israel.
18   How long he (work) for that firm? He says he (be) there since 1974.
19   You're looking tired. You not (have) a holiday for a long time?
20   Where you (be)? I not (see) you for ages.

Tense revision

Put the verbs in brackets into the correct form and fill in the blank spaces

Bill   You still (go) to night school, Mary?
Mary   Yes, of course. I (go) there for the last six months.
Bill   You (like) that school, ... you?
Mary   Yes, I . . . . . , very much. But I not (be) very good at German yet.
Bill   Neither . . . . . I, although I (study) it since last Easter.
Mary   That's not long. You (do) any exams yet?
Bill   No, I . . . . . I not (have) much chance to study.
Mary   By the way, who (teach) you last year?
Bill   I not (remember) his name. I not (see) him since the summer. Why?
Mary   He (be) German?

Bill   Yes, but he not (be) to Germany for three years.

Mary   Neither . . . . . my teacher. He says he not (be) to Germany
for five years. He must (be) homesick, ... he?

Bill   Perhaps he (prefer) London.

Unit 12

12.1 Reading

Whatever shall I do?

Mrs Turnbull	Oh, constable, something terrible's happened. I've lost my cat. He jumped out of the bedroom window into the garden, and I can't find him.
Policeman	I'm sure he'll come back soon.
Mrs Turnbull	No, he won't. He's never been out before and doesn't know where to go. It'll be dark soon. Whatever shall I do?
Policeman	Keep calm, madam. Sit down a moment, will you?
Mrs Turnbull	Calm? Sit down? How can I keep calm when my cat is missing? You don't seem to understand, constable, he'll be

	hungry soon because he hasn't eaten anything today. I don't know what he'll do.
Policeman	He'll come home, of course.
Mrs Turnbull	I don't think he'll ever come back.
Policeman	Of course he will. He'll come back if he wants to.
Mrs Turnbull	Anyway, what are you going to do about it?
Policeman	Shall I come back with you and look for him?
Mrs Turnbull	Oh thank you, constable. You *are* kind. But I don't think we'll find him.
Policeman	We can try, can't we? I'll just tell the Sergeant where I'm going. Wait here a moment, will you? I shan't be long.

Why can't Mrs Turnbull find her cat?
What's the policeman sure about?
Why is Mrs Turnbull so worried about her cat?
Why will the cat be hungry?
What does the policeman think the cat will do?
What does Mrs Turnbull think?
What will the cat do if he wants to?
What does the policeman offer to do?
What will the policeman do before he goes?
Will he be long?

12.2 Intonation

'Sit 'down for a moment, ⁄will you?
To make an imperative less of a command and more of a request or suggestion, add the tag: WILL YOU?
'Wait 'here a moment, ⁄will you?

The tag for imperatives and suggestions in the 1st person plural is SHALL WE?
'Let's 'go, ⁄shall we?
The voice falls on the imperative and rises again on the SHALL/WILL.

Ask someone or make a suggestion to do the following:
Pass the butter.
Let's go to the cinema.
Give me a cigarette.
Lend me your pen a moment.
Let's start.

69

Open the window.
Let's watch the match on the telly.
Write this down.
Let's go home now.
Give me a ring about six.
Let's do something else.

12.3 Oral practice

When will you see me again?
When will it be dark?
When will she be twenty-one?
When shall we see each other again?
What time will you get home tonight?
How will you get home?
Where will you be at this time tomorrow?
How long will it take you to learn English?
How long will it take you to get home?

Shall I open the window/shut the door?
Will you have a cigarette/drink/sweet/cup of tea?
Will you come to the cinema with me?

Offer me
a cup of tea/a sweet/a drink/a cigarette.
Offer to
open the window/close the door/help him/lend me some
money.

12.4 Listening comprehension

Peter meets Jim

Peter   Will you be at home later tonight, Jim?
Jim   I think so. Why?
Peter   There's something I want to ask you. I'll give you a ring
about eight, if that's all right with you.
Jim   Can't you tell me now?
Peter   I haven't time now. I'm going to the dentist's. He'll be
angry if I'm late.
Jim   I'll walk with you as far as the corner of the street.

Peter	It only takes a couple of minutes. He lives just round the corner.
Jim	I'll leave you here then.
Peter	All right. I'll ring you about eight then, shall I?
Jim	I'm very curious to know what it's about, Peter.
Peter	Oh, I only want to talk about our summer holidays.
Jim	Oh. As a matter of fact, I'm not sure if I'll be able to go away this year.
Peter	Why not?
Jim	Well, you know we've just bought a house, Peter, and what with one thing and another, I don't think we'll be able to afford it.
Peter	What a relief. Neither shall I. That's why I was going to ring you. To tell you I shan't be able to have a holiday either. I've just bought a car instead.
Jim	That's all right then, isn't it? You won't have to ring me up after all, will you?

When will Peter give Jim a ring?
Where's Peter going?
How long will it take him to get there?
Will the dentist be angry if he's late?
Where does the dentist live?
What does Peter want to talk to Jim about?
Why isn't Jim sure if he'll be able to go away this year?
Why was Peter going to ring him?
Why won't he have to ring him after all?

Who'll be home later tonight?
Who'll be angry if Peter is late?
Who won't be able to have a holiday?
Who won't have to ring Jim up after all?

Ask me if
Jim'll be home later.
Peter'll give him a ring about eight.
the dentist will be angry if he's late.
it'll take Peter a couple of minutes to get there.
Jim'll be able to go away this year.
he'll be able to afford a holiday.

Ask me
when he'll be home.

71

when he'll give him a ring.
how long it'll take him to get there.
why he won't be able to have a holiday this year.
why he won't have to ring him up after all.

12.5 Writing

Put the verbs in brackets into the SHALL/WILL DO *form where possible*
1 You (have) a cup of coffee?
2 They not (lend) him the money.
3 I (do) that for you?
4 It (be) time for lunch soon.
5 We (have to) do this again.
6 You (be able to) speak English well next year.
7 I never (get) there in time. I (take) a taxi?
8 He (do) it if they (pay) him.
9 I don't think they (pay) him.
10 Where we (go) tonight?
11 He isn't sure when he (be back).
12 We can't move into our new house until it (be) ready.
13 We can eat as soon as they (arrive).
14 I (do) it if I (have) the time.
15 They not (be) there when you (come).

Unit 13

13.1 Reading

How long will you be staying?

Simpson	Good evening. My name's Simpson. I booked a room by post about a month ago.
Clerk	Oh yes, sir. Here we are. How long will you be staying?
Simpson	Oh, only a couple of nights. Until I can find a room of my own.
Clerk	I see. Yes, that will be all right. Will you be eating your meals in the hotel?
Simpson	Only the evening meal. I'll be out looking for a room most of the day.

73

Clerk	Very good, sir. We'll be serving dinner in half an hour, sir.
Simpson	Oh good. I'll just go and have a bath and change.
Clerk	Oh, by the way, sir, a Miss Winters left a message for you. She asked me to tell you that she will be working late tonight so she won't be able to see you until tomorrow.
Simpson	Oh, I see.
Clerk	But she says she'll give you a ring about 8.30 tonight.
Simpson	I'll be having dinner at that time.
Clerk	That's all right, sir. We'll call you in the dining-room.
Simpson	Thanks a lot. Don't forget, will you? It's most important.

How long will Simpson be staying at the hotel?
Will he be eating in the hotel?
What will he be doing most of the day?
When will they be serving dinner?
Why won't Miss Winters be able to see him until tomorrow?
What will Simpson be doing when she rings him at 8.30?

13.2 Intonation

'Don't for`get, `will you?
When the voice falls both in the statement and the tag, the
negative imperative means: PLEASE don't forget.

Ask someone politely not to do the following:
Don't be late.
Don't go without me.
Don't forget to buy me some cigarettes.
Don't be too long.
Don't spend too much.
Don't lose your temper.
Don't lose it.

13.3 Oral practice

What will you be doing this weekend/time tomorrow?
Where will you be going for the weekend?
What will you be having for supper tonight?
Where will you be going for your holidays this year?
When will you be seeing me again?
When shall I be seeing you again?
When will you be having lunch?

74

Where will you be having lunch?
What time will you be going home?
How many more years will you be studying English?

Ask me if
I'll be going away for the weekend.
you'll be seeing me tomorrow.
I'll be going home by bus.
anybody'll be waiting for me at home.
I'll still be teaching English in ten years' time.
I'll be having lunch at one.

Ask me
what I'll be doing this time tomorrow.
where I'll be going for the weekend.
when you'll be seeing me again.
when I'll be having lunch.
what time I'll be going home.

13.4   Listening comprehension

Jean and Betty

Jean   Will you be seeing Tom tomorrow by any chance?
Betty   Tom? Tom who?
Jean   Tom Turner, of course. He's your boy-friend, isn't he?
Betty   I suppose so. Why do you want to know if I'll be seeing him
        tomorrow?
Jean   Because Harry's coming for a meal tomorrow night, and I
        wanted to ask you and Tom as well.
Betty   Oh, I see. As a matter of fact, I shan't be here. I'm going
        away for the weekend.
Jean   Will Tom be going with you?
Betty   No. He's got to work late at the office, so he'll be staying in
        town till Saturday.
Jean   Shall I ask him round later?
Betty   If you want to. He'll be happy to come, I'm sure.
Jean   As long as you don't mind.
Betty   Not at all. I'll be only too pleased to know he'll be with you
        and Harry.

When's Harry coming for a meal?

Why does Jean want to know if Betty will be seeing Tom
tomorrow?
Why won't Betty be there?
Will Tom be going with her?
Why won't he be going with her?
How long will he be staying in town for?
Why doesn't Betty mind if Jean asks him to come?

Who's Betty's boy-friend?
Who's coming for a meal tomorrow night?
Who won't be here?
Who'll be staying in town until Saturday?

Ask me if
she'll be seeing him tomorrow night.
he'll be going for a meal tomorrow night.
she won't be there.
he'll be staying in town.
she minds if he goes.

Ask me
when she'll be seeing him.
where he'll be going for a meal.
who Betty's boy-friend is.
why she won't be here.
why he won't be going with her.
how long he'll be staying in town.

13.5   Writing

Put the verbs in brackets into the correct form: SHALL/WILL *be doing.*
1   I expect he (work) late tonight.
2   He not (work) when I go to see him.
3   You (have) lunch with me today?
4   We (eat) soon.
5   When you (see) Janet again?
6   I (think) of you while you are on holiday.
7   My daughter not (come) for the weekend because she's ill.
8   They not (go) to Turkey again this year.
9   She not (play) tennis this afternoon?
10 They not (use) the car again today?

Unit 14

14.1 Reading

Simpson's future landlady

Landlady	This is your room, Mr Simpson. Do you like it?
Simpson	Er – it looks very nice. But it's a bit small, isn't it?
Landlady	Small, but cosy. Will you be staying long?
Simpson	I'll be staying a couple of months.
Landlady	I see. I usually let this room to a girl. This is the first time I've let it to a man.
Simpson	I haven't taken it yet.
Landlady	I thought you said you liked the room.

Simpson	I do. But I'll have to think about it first.
Landlady	Well, don't take too long, will you? I can't keep it free indefinitely.
Simpson	I'll let you know this afternoon.
Landlady	I see. I suppose you're going to look at other places first and compare.
Simpson	Er – yes, I am. In fact, I'm seeing another place at midday.
Landlady	Well, you won't find anything as cheap as this.
Simpson	No, I suppose not. It's just that it's a long way from work.
Landlady	The bus service is very good.
Simpson	Is it? Well, anyway, I'll ring you this afternoon.
Landlady	I'm not on the phone. It's too expensive.
Simpson	Oh. In that case, I'll come back about four, if that's all right with you.
Landlady	Perfectly all right. I'll be here.

How long will he be staying if he takes the room?
When will he let her know?
What's he going to do first?
What's he doing at midday?
Will he find anything cheaper, according to the landlady?
When does he say he will ring her?
What time will he come back?
Where will the landlady be?

14.2 Intonation

It ˈlooks very ˌnice (but it's a bit small).
When you have doubts about something or do not completely
agree with somebody, use the falling–rising tune.

Try to do it. I'll ˇtry (but I don't think I can).
The sign ˇ is used when the voice falls and rises in the same
word.

Agree reluctantly or have doubts about the following:

Someone says	*You say*	*You mean*
He'll help you.	I ˈhope he ˌwill.	(but I have my doubts)
He's very clever, isn't he?	He ˈworks very ˌhard.	(but clever, no)

78

You like him, don't ˇYes.   (but not much)
you?

Are you warm   I'm not ˇcold.   (but I'm not hot
enough?   either)

Can I borrow your   You 'can if you   (but I'm not happy
car?   ˇlike.   about it)

Can you come   Toˇmorrow?   (that's difficult)
tomorrow?

What's he like?   He's good-   (but that's about
    ˇlooking.   all)

Do you like my   It's a 'nice ˇcolour.   (but a terrible
new dress?   design)

Are you coming to   Yes, I'm ˇcoming.   (but I don't want to)
the party?

You smacked my   I'm ˇsorry.   (but he deserved it)
child.

14.3   Oral practice (See Summary 14)

The teacher reads the statements, and the student transforms
them to the correct tense to express a future action.

(1) Teacher   We've arranged to watch television tonight.
    Student   *We're watching* television tonight.
(2) Teacher   We intend to watch television tonight.
    Student   *We're going to watch* television tonight.
(3) Teacher   We've just decided to watch television tonight.
    Student   *We'll watch* television tonight.
(4) Teacher   As usual, we'll watch television tonight.
    Student   *We'll be watching* television tonight.

They've arranged to do it.   (1)
They intend to do it.   (2)
They've just decided to do it.   (3)
They're doing it as usual.   (4)

He usually sees her home after the lesson.   (4)
He intends to see her home after the lesson.   (2)
He's arranged to see her home after the lesson.   (1)
He's decided to see her home after the lesson.   (3)

I've arranged to lend you the money.   (1)
I'm lending you the money as I always do.   (4)

| I intend to lend you the money. | (2) |
| I've decided to lend you the money. | (3) |

She's working late tonight as usual.	(4)
She intends to work late tonight.	(2)
She's decided to work late tonight.	(3)
She's arranged to work late tonight.	(1)

We've decided not to watch television tonight.	(3)
We won't watch television tonight as we usually do.	(4)
We've arranged not to watch television tonight.	(1)
We intend not to watch television tonight.	(2)

They have no intention of doing it.	(2)
They've decided not to do it, after all.	(3)
They've arranged not to do it.	(1)
They're not doing it as they usually do.	(4)

14.4   Listening comprehension

Bill and Harry

Bill   What's the date today?
Harry   It's the 23rd. Why?
Bill   My birthday's on the 27th. I'd almost forgotten.
Harry   How old will you be?
Bill   I'll be twenty-five.
Harry   Are you having a birthday party?
Bill   Yes, of course. Won't you be coming?
Harry   You haven't asked me yet.
Bill   I'm asking you now. By the way, will you be seeing Janet before then?
Harry   Yes, I will. Do you want her to come too?
Bill   Yes, but I don't know her address.
Harry   Shall I ask her for you? I'll be seeing her tomorrow evening.
Bill   That's a good idea. Will you ask her to bring some of her records with her? She's got a marvellous collection.
Harry   You seem to know an awful lot about my girl-friend.
Bill   Don't be so suspicious. Remember, she used to work in my office, so I got to know her quite well.
Harry   Well, all I can say is I'm glad she changed her job. I'm going to marry her, you know.

What had Bill almost forgotten?
When is his birthday?
How old will he be on the 27th?
Is he having a birthday party?
Will Harry be seeing Janet before the 27th?
When will he be seeing her?
What does Harry offer to do?
What does Bill want her to bring?
How did Bill get to know Janet?
What's Harry going to do?

Who'll be twenty-five on the 27th?
Who's having a birthday party?
Who'll be seeing Janet tomorrow evening?
Who's got a marvellous collection of records?
Who used to work with Bill?
Who's going to marry Harry?

Ask me if
he'll be twenty-five on the 27th.
he'll be coming to the party.
he'll be seeing Janet before then.
he's going to marry her.

Ask me
how old he'll be on the 27th.
when he's having a party.
when he'll be seeing Janet.
who he's going to marry.

14.5   Writing

Revision: Put the verbs in brackets into the correct form
I (walk) along the road the other day when I (meet) an old
girl-friend of mine. She (wear) a fur coat and (look) very
prosperous.
   'What you (do) these days?' I (ask) her.
   'I just (finish) making my first film', she (say). 'Everyone
(think) it (be) a great success when it (come out). In my next
film I (play) the lead.'
   'I not (know) you (want) to be an actress', I (answer).
'How long you (work) in films?'

81

'I not (act) for very long', she (reply). 'But when I (be) in Rome last summer, I (fall in love) with a film producer.'

'That (be) lucky, not (be) it?' I (say) rather bitterly.

'What you (mean) by lucky?' she (reply), angrily. 'I (work) hard to become an actress.'

I (feel) bitter, because I always (want) to be an actor but I never (have) the opportunity. I (be in love) with that girl five years ago. I always (like) her, and although I (feel) a little jealous at the moment, I (know) I always (feel) something for her.

Unit 15

15.1 Reading

What would you like for supper?

Landlady	What would you like for supper tonight, Mr Simpson?
Simpson	What do you suggest?
Landlady	Well now, let's see. Would you like scrambled eggs on toast?
Simpson	No thanks. You gave me an omelette for lunch.
Landlady	So I did. Well, would you like a nice salad, or would you rather have a bowl of soup?
Simpson	Er – I'd rather have a pork chop, or sausages and chips. Something like that.
Landlady	I'm sure you would, Mr Simpson. But meat is very expensive,

	you know. And with the low rent you're paying . . . What
	would you say to biscuits and cheese?
Simpson	I'd say it wouldn't be enough.
Landlady	There's no need to be rude, Mr Simpson.
Simpson	Sorry. Anyway, give me what you like.
Landlady	A nice hot cup of tea then. Or would you rather have
	cocoa?
Simpson	Whichever is cheaper.
Landlady	I shan't be long. (*She goes*)
Simpson	I wish she'd give me something to eat now and then.

Why wouldn't Mr Simpson like scrambled eggs on toast?
What else does she offer him?
What would he rather have?
Would biscuits and cheese be enough for him?
What does he wish?

15.2 Intonation

I `wish she'd give me something to ˌeat.

I WISH + WOULD expresses a strong desire that *someone else* will do something *in the future*, but you know that this is not likely to happen. Compare with 11.2.

'I'm not coming to your party.'
'I `wish you ˌwould.' / 'I `wish you'd ˌcome.'

The fall is on WISH, and the rise on the second part of the sentence.

You are thinking: She's not coming to my party.
You say: I `wish she'd come to my ˌparty.

Wish the following in the same way:
You aren't listening to me.
They haven't paid me.
He won't go.
He never rings me up.
He never asks me out to dinner.
Please speak to him about it.
Why doesn't she hurry up?

Why won't he switch the radio off?
Will it never stop raining?
He smokes too much.

15.3   Oral practice

Teacher   Would you like to live in London?
Student   Yes, I would./No, I wouldn't.
Teacher   Would you like to have dinner with me?
Student   Yes, I'd like to very much. Thank you./
           I'm awfully sorry, I can't. Thanks all the same.
Teacher   Would you like a sweet?
Student   Yes please./No thanks.
Teacher   Would you like a cup of tea or would you rather have a
           coffee?
Student   I'd rather have a cup of tea (coffee).

a)
Would you like a sweet/cigarette/drink/cup of tea/coffee?
Would you like to live in London/Rome/Paris/New York?
Would you like to study Russian/write a book/have a lot of
money?
Would you like to/have dinner with me?
                 /come to the theatre with me?
                 /come to the cinema with me?

b)
Would you like a cup of tea or would you rather have a
coffee?
Which would she rather have?
Would you like a sweet or would you rather have a
chocolate?
Which would she rather have?
Would you like a beer or would you rather have a Scotch?
Which would he rather have?
Would you like to go to the States for a holiday or would
you rather go to India?
Where would he rather go?
Would you rather go in the summer or in the winter?
When would he rather go?

Offer me a cigarette/drink/sweet etc.

85

Offer me a cup of tea or a coffee/a sweet or a chocolate/a
beer or a Scotch.

Ask me
if I'd like to/live in London/Rome/Paris/etc.
/study Russian/write a book/
/have a lot of money.
to dinner/the theatre/the cinema.
out to dinner or to lunch/to the theatre or the cinema.
which I'd rather do/have.
if I'd like to go to the States or if I'd rather go to India.
if I'd rather go in the summer or in the winter.
when I'd rather go.
where I'd rather go.

15.4   Listening comprehension

Hugh and Wendy in the garden

Hugh	It's a fabulous day, Wendy. Would you like to go for a drive?
Wendy	Yes, I would, very much. But the roads will be very crowded. It's Sunday, you know.
Hugh	It doesn't matter. It would be good for us to get some fresh air.
Wendy	There won't be much fresh air with all those cars on the road.
Hugh	Oh, come on. A drive would do you good.
Wendy	I'd rather stay at home, if you don't mind. I'd like to do some gardening.
Hugh	Well, I'd rather go for a drive.
Wendy	Well, we're not going, and that's that. I'm going to do some gardening. Wouldn't you like to help me?
Hugh	Not much. It's too hot.
Wendy	Oh, come on. I wish you'd stop complaining all the time. I'll make a nice cup of tea in a minute. Would you like that?
Hugh	I'd rather have a beer.
Wendy	Have what you want. And I wish you'd take your coat off. You'll die in this heat.

What does Hugh ask Wendy?
What would be good for them?
Why doesn't she want to go for a drive?
What would she rather do?
What would Hugh rather do?

What's Wendy going to do?
Why wouldn't Hugh like to help her in the garden?
What does Wendy wish he'd stop doing?
What does she offer him?
What would he rather have?
What does she wish he'd do?

Ask me if
she'd like to go for a drive.
it'd be good for them.
a drive would do her good.
she'd rather stay at home.
she'd like to do some gardening.
he'd rather go for a drive.
he'd like a cup of tea.
he'd rather have a beer.

Ask me
what would be good for them.
what would do Wendy good.
what she'd rather do.
what she'd like to do at home.
what Hugh would rather do.
why Hugh wouldn't like to help her.
what he'd rather have.

15.5 Writing

Put the verbs in brackets into the correct form: WOULD DO/WOULD
LIKE/WOULD RATHER
1 What you (like) to drink?
2 He (like) to go for a drive but she (prefer) stay at home.
3 You (like) something to eat?
4 He (want) to speak to you personally.
5 If you don't mind, I not (prefer) go out tonight.
6 You (like) to come for a walk? The fresh air (be) good
   for you.
7 I not (want) to annoy her.
8 You (like) to go to the pictures, or you (prefer) watch telly?
9 I wish they (hurry up).
10 I wish you not (blow) smoke in my face.

Unit 16

16.1 Reading

What would you do if you won the Pools?

Fred   If I won the Pools, I'd go round the world.
Bert   Would you? I wouldn't.
Fred   What would you do?
Bert   Oh, I don't know. I'd buy a big house with a garden for the
wife and kids, I suppose. But it's difficult to imagine having a
lot of money.
Fred   One thing's certain. If I had a lot of money, I wouldn't
work any more.

88

Bert	Wouldn't you? What would you do with all that spare time?
Fred	As I said, I'd go round the world.
Bert	What would you do after that?
Fred	Oh, I don't know. It'd take me a long time to go round the world.
Bert	It doesn't sound very exciting.
Fred	Anyway, we haven't won the Pools, and we're not likely to win them. So there isn't much point in talking about it, is there?
Bert	I'd be happy if I got a rise.
Fred	And my wife would be happy if I bought her a mink coat.
Bert	Well, I'm not likely to get a rise and you haven't the money for a mink coat, so let's come down to earth and have another drink.
Fred	What'll you have?
Bert	I'll have a pint of the best.
Fred	I'd have a Scotch if I were you. We deserve it.
Bert	All right. Make it a double, will you?

What would Fred do if he won the Pools?
What would Bert buy if he won the Pools?
Who would he buy the house and garden for?
Would Fred stop working if he had a lot of money?
What would he do with his spare time?
How long would it take Fred to go round the world?
What would make Bert happy?
What would make Fred's wife happy?
What does Fred advise Bert to drink?

16.2 Intonation

'I'd have a `Scotch, if ‚I were you.
WOULD + IF I WERE YOU expresses strong advice or even a command.
The fall is in the first phrase, with the rise beginning on the second I.

Why don't you go? I'd `go if 'I were you.
Don't go.   I `wouldn't go if ‚I were you.
Transform the following the same way:

Why don't you stay?

89

Why don't you marry him?
Don't stay.
Don't smoke so much.
Why don't you ask her out to dinner?
Don't buy it.
Why don't you accept their invitation?
Don't eat at that restaurant.
Why don't you have something to eat before the journey?
Don't do it.
Why don't you take an umbrella?
Don't drink any more.

16.3 Oral practice

Would you be annoyed if your wife bought a fur coat?
Would you be angry if someone stole your car?
Would you be pleased if someone gave you a present?
Would you be glad if you stopped work?
Would you be delighted if your parents bought you a car?

How would you feel if someone
stole your car?
broke your pen?
hit your child?
did all your work for you?
gave you a present?
bought you a fur coat/car/piano/motor-bike/guitar?

What did he say?   What would you do if you had a lot of money?
Would you stop work if you had the chance?
Would you lend me/him some money if I/he asked you?
Would you live abroad if you had the money?
If your firm offered you a job abroad, would you take it?

Transform like this:
Teacher   I'll go if she asks me.
1st Student   What did he say?
2nd Student   He said he'd go if she asked him.

He'll do it if you pay him enough.
I'll be there in five minutes if I take a taxi.
She'll marry him if he asks her.

90

They'll lend me the money if I need it.
You'll speak English well if you work hard.
You'll learn English quickly if you live in Britain.
He'll ring her up if he wants to.
We'll go if we have the time.
You'll feel better if you smoke less.
She'll get wet if it rains.
He won't drive if it's foggy.
They won't come if she's there.
I won't help him even if he pays me.
He won't do it even if you pay him.
She won't marry him even if he asks her.
They won't lend me the money even if I need it.

16.4 Listening comprehension

George asks Anne out

George	Hello. Is that you, Anne?
Anne	Oh, it's you, is it?
George	Yes, it is. Aren't you pleased to speak to me?
Anne	Yes, of course. But I wish you wouldn't ring me up at the same time every evening. It's so monotonous.
George	Oh, sorry. I only wanted to know – would you like to come out with me tomorrow night?
Anne	Where to?
George	Would you like to see the film at our local? It's a musical.
Anne	I'd rather go to town and see a good play.
George	Oh, all right. It costs more, you know.
Anne	Well, of course, if you can't afford it.
George	It isn't that.
Anne	What then?
George	I wish you'd be more enthusiastic sometimes.
Anne	I'd be more enthusiastic if you behaved yourself when we go out.
George	What do you mean?
Anne	Well, you always want to talk about love and romance. Why can't you be more practical sometimes? I'd be more down to earth if I were you.
George	I *am* down to earth. As a matter of fact, I'm going to ask you something special.
Anne	What?

George	Well – would you marry me if I asked you?
Anne	You haven't asked me yet.
George	Well, I'm going to ask you tomorrow night. I'll pick you up at the office about six. All right?
Anne	All right.

What does Anne wish George wouldn't do?
What did George want to know?
What would he like to see?
What would Anne rather do?
What does George wish she'd be?
What would make Anne more enthusiastic?
What's George going to ask her tomorrow night?

Who'd like to see the musical?
Who'd rather see a good play?

Ask me if
she'd like to go out with him.
she'd like to see the film at the local cinema.
she'd rather go to town.
she'd be more enthusiastic if he behaved himself.
she'd marry him if he asked her.

Ask me
where he would like to go.
what he would like to see.
what Anne would rather do.
where she'd rather go.
what'd make her more enthusiastic.

16.5   Writing

Put the verbs in brackets into the correct form
1   You (feel) better if you took your medicine.
2   She would come to the party if he (be) there.
3   He would help you if he (be able to).
4   If he (need) the money, would you give it to him?
5   If they paid me enough, I (accept) the job.
6   I'd walk home if there (be) a bus strike.
7   I'd do it if I (have to).
8   If he had a better salary, he (go) abroad every year.

9   I not (go) even if I had enough money.
10 He (ring) me up if he wanted to.

Unit 17

17.1 Reading

You should see a doctor

Peter	Look at your face. It's covered in spots.
Alice	Let me see. My God, I've got chickenpox.
Peter	Measles. You'd better call the doctor immediately.
Alice	But I feel all right. I think I'll wait till tonight.
Peter	Don't be silly. You should see a doctor at once. I could take you in the car.
Alice	I'd have to make an appointment first if I wanted to see him this morning.

Peter	Well, make one then. Ring him up now. You should think of other people now and then.
Alice	All right, all right. Calm down. You ought to go to the doctor's yourself, your nerves are in such a state. Could you give me his number, please?
Peter	Isn't it in your diary? You should write these things down.
Alice	It'll be in the phone book. Anyway, if I went to see him now, I'd have to put off Henri. He should be here any minute.
Peter	Who on earth's he?
Alice	He's a famous make-up artist. I'm sure he'd be able to cover up my spots with something if I asked him.

What had Alice better do?
When should she see a doctor?
What could Peter do?
What would she have to do if she wanted to see the doctor this morning?
Who should she think of now and then?
Why does Alice say he ought to go to the doctor's himself?
What should Alice write down in her diary?
What would she have to do if she went to see the doctor now?
Who should be here any minute?
What is she sure Henri would be able to do?

17.2 Intonation

I've got chickenpox. Measles.

When you want to correct what someone has just said, the voice falls then rises quickly on the same word.

This is the same as when you contradict somebody (see 6.2), but the fall–rise is on one word only.

Wendy is telling a friend about her neighbours next door, but either she gets her facts wrong or she exaggerates a little. Her husband, Hugh, corrects her.

Read the part of Hugh.

Wendy	They told me they were married in Westminster Abbey.
Hugh	St ˅Paul's.
Wendy	And that their son John—
Hugh	˅Jack.

95

Wendy   —went to school at Eton.
Hugh   ⱽHarrow.
Wendy   And then to Oxford—
Hugh   ⱽCambridge.
Wendy   —where he got a degree in history.
Hugh   ⱽEnglish.
Wendy   And now he's teaching in Edinburgh.
Hugh   ⱽGlasgow.
Wendy   She says he's writing a book about Shakespeare.
Hugh   ⱽMarlowe.
Wendy   He's only twenty-four.
Hugh   ⱽTwenty-six.
Wendy   Anyway, he got married last year.
Hugh   The year beⱽfore.
Wendy   And they went on their honeymoon for three months.
Hugh   ⱽTwo.
Wendy   They toured Greece.
Hugh   ⱽItaly.
Wendy   Then they took a house by the sea.
Hugh   A ⱽflat.
Wendy   I don't know how they can afford it.
Hugh   ˋI ˏdo. His wife's very good with money.

17.3   Oral practice

a)

What did   Should I/ought I to/had I better/ask him a question?
I ask?   /lend him the money?
                                    /ask them to my party?
                                    /see the new film at the Odeon?
                                    /explain this to you again?

What did   Should we/ought we to/had we better/do this again?
I ask?   /study it at home?
                                    /speak English in class?
                                    /stop for a break now?
                                    /get here on time?

b)

What did   If you lived abroad, would you have to/learn the language?
he say?   /find a job?
                                    /send money home?

What did *he say?*	If you had a lot of money, would you have to/work? /get up early? /learn English?

What did *he say?*	If you went on holiday tomorrow, would you have to book in advance? tell your wife first? tell your parents? go to the bank first? pack a suitcase?

c)

What did *I ask?*	Could you/speak a little faster? /speak English in class? /come here tomorrow? /give me a cigarette, please?

d)

What did *he say?*	If you had a lot of money, would you be able to stop work? go round the world? do what you like?

What did *he say?*	If you lived in England, would you be able to speak English well? find a job easily? send money home?

17.4 Listening comprehension

George and Anne on the way to the theatre

George   Have you thought over what I asked you yesterday?
Anne   What was that?
George   You know quite well what it was. I asked you if you'd marry me.
Anne   You didn't *ask* me. You said you *would* ask me. There's a difference. So you'd better ask me, hadn't you?
George   Should I get down on my knees or something?
Anne   You'd better not. People would stare. Couldn't you wait until we're in a more romantic place?
George   But you said I should be more down to earth.

97

Anne	So I did. But you'd better hurry up, or we'll be late.
George	Very well. Anne, will you marry me?
Anne	I don't know.
George	What do you mean, you don't know?
Anne	What I said. I'll have to ask my parents first.
George	What for? You're over twenty-one.
Anne	That's not the point. I ought to tell them first.
George	Tell them, yes. Not ask them.
Anne	Anyway, I'd have to think about it first before I took such a big decision. I'm not at all sure I could live with someone like you.
George	What's wrong with me?
Anne	You're too practical and down to earth. You should be more romantic sometimes. There's a time and a place for everything.

What did George ask Anne?
What had he better ask her?
What had he better not do?
Why doesn't Anne want him to get down on his knees?
What did Anne tell George he should be?
Why had he better hurry up?
Who would she have to tell before she decided?
What would she have to do before she took such a big decision?
What isn't she sure about?
What does she suggest he should be sometimes?

Ask me if
he should/had better ask her to marry him.
he should/ought to/had better get down on his knees.
he could wait/couldn't wait for a while.
she should/ought to tell her parents first.
she'd have to think about it.
she could live with him.

Ask me
what George had better ask Anne.
what he should do.
what he ought to do.
why he couldn't wait.
what she'd have to do before she took such a big decision.
why she couldn't live with him.

17.5 Writing

Put SHOULD/OUGHT TO/HAD BETTER/WOULD HAVE TO/COULD *or*
WOULD BE ABLE TO *into the blank spaces.*
(Some sentences can have two forms, depending on the
meaning.)

1 I . . . . . do some work, but I don't want to.
2 He . . . . . go to bed if he doesn't feel well.
3 If I went by train, I . . . . . leave at eight.
4 If he asked me to lend him some money, I . . . . . refuse.
5 If you don't know the answer, you . . . . . tell me.
6 He . . . . . be able to answer that question.
7 . . . . . you ask him to wait for me, please?
8 We . . . . . go to the art exhibition, if you like.
9 They . . . . . be able to speak English well by now.
10 You . . . . . go to the States if you won the first prize.
11 He . . . . . find it if he put on his glasses.
12 They . . . . . get a visa if they went to Russia.
13 We . . . . . see better if you switched on the light.
14 You . . . . . be able to find a job easily with your
   qualifications.
15 If we go to the theatre, we . . . . . book our seats in
   advance.
16 I . . . . . see you tonight, if you like.
17 He . . . . . answer that if he were here.
18 It . . . . . n't be difficult to do that.
19 Even if I came to your party, I . . . . . leave early.
20 I . . . . . repair it if I knew how it worked.

Unit 18

18.1 Reading

You should have gone to the doctor's

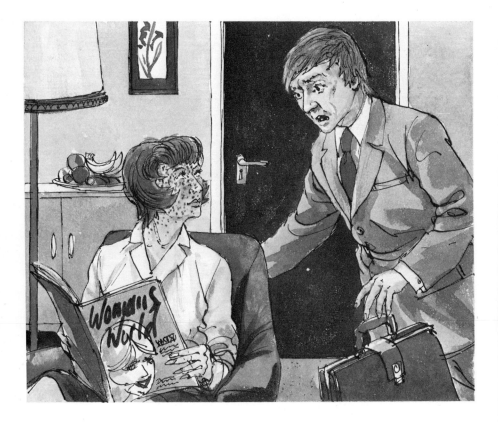

Peter   My God, your face is worse than ever. Didn't you go to the doctor's this morning?

Alice   I didn't have time.

Peter   You should have made time. I told you to go. You should have rung him up at once.

Alice   Yes, I suppose I ought to have. I'll go later this evening.

Peter   You shouldn't have wasted all this time. Why couldn't you

	have gone this morning? What have you been doing since I left you?
Alice	I told you. I had an appointment with Henri, the beautician.
Peter	That couldn't have taken all day.
Alice	It didn't. He should have come at eleven o'clock, but he didn't turn up till ten past twelve. And by the time he had finished, it was lunch-time.
Peter	Finished what?
Alice	My face, of course.
Peter	It's a pity he couldn't have made a better job of it.
Alice	Actually, he didn't do anything in the end because of the spots. He said it would be too dangerous.
Peter	I could have told him that.
Alice	So we just sat and talked.
Peter	Oh, you did, did you?
Alice	He said I ought to have seen him years ago. He could have done so much to help my skin.
Peter	Oh, he could, could he?
Alice	So he's taking me to a skin specialist tomorrow.

Who ought Alice to have rung?
What shouldn't she have wasted?
What does Peter want to know?
What couldn't have taken all day?
When should Henri have come?
What does Peter think is a pity?
What could Peter have told him?
Why should Alice have seen Henri years ago?

18.2 Intonation

We sat and talked.
Oh, you `did, ,did you?
He could have done so much to help my skin.
Oh, he `could, ,could he?

To sound sarcastic, the voice falls on the first auxiliary and rises on the second.

Hugh is late for dinner, and Wendy has been waiting for him. She is not at all pleased.
Read the part of Wendy.

Hugh	I'm sorry I'm late—
Wendy	Oh, you are, are you?
Hugh	—but I met George. We went to our local for a drink.
Wendy	Oh, you did, did you?
Hugh	I was going to ring you—
Wendy	Oh, you were, were you?
Hugh	—but you wouldn't have come anyway, would you?
Wendy	Oh, I wouldn't, wouldn't I?
Hugh	Gosh, I'm hungry. I could eat a three-course meal.
Wendy	Oh, you could, could you?
Hugh	Well, I've only had a sandwich today.
Wendy	Oh, you have, have you?
Hugh	What's the matter with you? You sound bad-tempered and irritable.
Wendy	Oh, I do, do I?
Hugh	You should take a tranquillizer.
Wendy	Oh, I should, should I?

18.3   Oral practice

a)
Duty or action not done

Teacher	Did you get up early this morning?
Student	No. I should have got up early, but I didn't./ No. I ought to have got up early, but I didn't.

The more natural reply would be: No, I should have done, but I didn't. This exercise is to elicit the Past Participle of the verb as well.
Make sure the students say SHOULD'VE and not SHOULD HAVE.

Did you do your homework last night?
Did you go to see the film at the Odeon?
Did you have breakfast this morning?
Did you study this at home?
Did she ring you up last night?
Did he ask you out to dinner?
Did I explain this to you last week?
Did she meet you yesterday afternoon?

Did you come to my lesson last week?
Did you make an appointment to see the dentist?

b)
Disapproval of a past action

Teacher   I lost my temper.
Student   You shouldn't have lost your temper./
            You oughtn't to have lost your temper.

Make sure the students say SHOULDN'T'VE and not SHOULDN'T
HAVE.

I went to the party without being asked.
I rang her up after midnight.
I smoked a cigarette in class.
He hit me.
He broke his promise.
She refused to speak to him.
They were very rude to me.
You were making fun of me.
You did it.
I bought them a present.
You ate too much.
We drank too much last night.
She married him.

c)
Ability unfulfilled

Teacher   Were you able to go yesterday?
Student   I could have gone, but I didn't.

Make sure the students say COULD'VE and not COULD HAVE.

Were you/they able to/play tennis yesterday?
                       /go away for the weekend?
                       /speak to him?
                       /do your/their homework?
                       /have a holiday?
                       /buy it?

Was he/she able to/help you?
                    /be there?
                    /ring you up?
                    /lend you the money?
                    /tell you before?

d)
Contradiction or negative deduction

Teacher	He went to the cinema yesterday.
Student	He couldn't have gone, because he was ill.

Make sure the students say COULDN'T'VE and not COULDN'T HAVE.

He went to the theatre last night.
She/they/he/played tennis yesterday.
                    /went away for the weekend.
                    /came to the lesson yesterday.
                    /had a party last night.
                    /had a singing lesson yesterday.
                    /bought a new coat today.
                    /took her out to dinner last night.
                    /went shopping this morning.
I saw her in the street this morning.
I heard him singing in his bath.
I watched the President of the United States live on TV last night.
I listened to the Prime Minister on the radio this morning.

18.4   Listening comprehension

George finally gets an answer from Anne

Anne	What's the matter with you? Didn't you enjoy the play?
George	No, I thought it was awful. We should have gone to the musical.
Anne	Don't be so selfish. It was a marvellous play. It was a pity we missed the beginning, though. We shouldn't have been so late.
George	It wasn't my fault. We could have got there on time, but you insisted on eating first.

Anne	Well, I was hungry. I couldn't have sat through that play without eating something.
George	You could have had a sandwich or something instead of a three-course meal. I'm sure you couldn't have been *that* hungry.
Anne	Why not? I hadn't eaten since breakfast. Anyway, I paid for it, didn't I? So why should you worry?
George	I'm not worried.
Anne	Yes, you are. You're bad-tempered and irritable. You should have taken a tranquillizer before you came out.
George	It isn't a tranquillizer I need. It's a straight answer to my question.
Anne	Which one?
George	You know very well which one. For the last time, will you marry me?
Anne	I suppose so. But you could have asked me at a better time.
George	When would have been a better time?
Anne	You could have asked me while we were having dinner. We could have discussed our future instead of going to that silly play.

What did George think of the play?
According to George, where should they have gone?
What couldn't Anne have done without eating something first?
What could Anne have had instead of a three-course meal?
Who paid for it?
Why should George have taken a tranquillizer before he came out?
What did George ask her for the last time?
When should he have asked her to marry him?
What could they have talked about during dinner if he had asked her then?

Ask me if
they should have gone to the musical instead.
they could have got there on time.
she couldn't have had a sandwich instead.
he should've taken a tranquillizer before coming out.
he could've asked her at a better time.
he shouldn't have asked her during dinner.
they couldn't have discussed their future instead of going to the play.

Ask me
where they should've gone to instead.
why they couldn't have got there on time.
what she couldn't have done.
why she couldn't have been that hungry.
what he should've taken before coming out.
when he could've asked her.
when he should've asked her.
what they could have discussed.

18.5 Writing

Put SHOULD HAVE/OUGHT TO HAVE *or* COULD HAVE *into the blank spaces and change the verb in brackets to the correct form*

1 I . . . . . (meet) her yesterday, but I forgot.
2 You . . . . . not (hit) him so hard.
3 Hurry up. We're late already. You know we . . . . . (be) there by now.
4 I think you . . . . . (talk) it over with him first.
5 I'm not surprised you feel ill. You . . . . . not (eat) that so quickly.
6 Why didn't you ring me? We . . . . . (go) together.
7 They . . . . . not (watch) TV last night because their set's broken.
8 Why have you been so long? It . . . . . not (take) an hour to go to the grocer's and back.
9 I . . . . . not (walk) past him without speaking, could I?
10 I think we . . . . . (say) something.

Unit 19

19.1 Reading

I'd have eaten it all if I'd been hungry

Landlady	You haven't had much lunch, Mr Simpson. Don't you like my cooking?
Simpson	Oh yes, but to tell the truth, I wasn't very hungry.
Landlady	I wouldn't have made such a big stew if I had known that.
Simpson	Please don't take offence. I'd have eaten it all if I'd been hungry, but as I said, I wasn't.
Landlady	I see. Perhaps next time you'll let me know beforehand. By the way, are you going away for the weekend?

Simpson	No, I don't think so. I'd go if I had the time, but I've got to study for an exam.
Landlady	I see. Only you went away last weekend and didn't tell me in advance. You should have given me more warning.
Simpson	I'm sorry. I would have told you earlier if I'd known, but I wasn't invited till the last minute.
Landlady	I wouldn't have bought so much food last Saturday if you had told me in time. Fair's fair.
Simpson	I can only say that if I'd had enough money last week I'd have found a flat of my own, and then I would never have come back at all.

What wouldn't the landlady have done if she had known he wasn't hungry?
Would he have eaten it all if he had been hungry?
What would he do if he had the time?
What should he have done?
What would he have done if he had known he was going away for the weekend?
Would she have bought so much food if she had known in time?
What would he have done last week if he'd had enough money?

19.2 Intonation

I would have 'told you `earlier if I'd ,known.

In conditional sentences (sentences with IF) the voice usually falls on the most important word in the main part of the sentence, and rises on the most important word in the part which follows IF.
If I 'won the ,Pools, I'd 'go round the `world.

Say the following in the same way:
I'd go if I had the time.
I'd have eaten it all if I'd been hungry.
I'd be happy if I got a rise in salary.
If I won the Pools I'd go on a cruise.
I'll help her if she asks me.
If you don't take your medicine you won't get better.
I'd do it if I had to.

If I had a lot of money, I'd stop work.
If I'd had enough money, I'd have found a flat of my own.
I'll be there in five minutes if I take a taxi.
We'll go if it stops raining.

19.3 Oral practice

What did Would you
he say? have/gone to university/   if you'd had the chance?
            /learned to play the piano/
            /gone to England last year/
What did When you were on holiday last summer,
he say? would you have been/fed up if it had rained all the time?
                              /annoyed if you had lost all your money?
                              /pleased if you'd been able to stay
                                  longer?
                              /glad if it had cost less?
What did How would you have felt if/the food had been bad?
he say?   /it had rained all the time?
                                       /you had lost all your money?
                                       /the holiday had been free?

Transform

Teacher   I wanted to go, but he didn't ask me.
Student   You would have gone if he had asked you.
          (You'd've gone if he'd asked you.)
Teacher   You didn't want to go, so he didn't ask you.
Student   I wouldn't have gone even if he had asked me.
          (I wouldn't've gone even if he'd asked me.)

We wanted to go, but we didn't have the time.
He wanted to do it, but they didn't pay him enough.
She wanted to marry him, but he didn't ask her.
She knew she'd get wet if it rained, but it didn't rain.

You didn't want to help him, so he didn't ask you.
I knew they didn't want to lend me the money, so I didn't
ask them.
I knew they wouldn't come even if she were there.

19.4 Listening comprehension

Simpson gives in his notice

Landlady   Mr Simpson, you should have told me you were going away for the weekend.

Simpson   I'd have told you earlier if I'd known, but I was only invited at the last minute.

Landlady   I wouldn't have bought so much food if I'd known.

Simpson   I'm very sorry. As a matter of fact, I've got something else to tell you. I'll be leaving at the end of the week.

Landlady   Oh, you will, will you? You have to give me a month's notice, you know.

Simpson   I'll pay you the full amount, don't worry.

Landlady   I'm not worried. You young people are all the same. You think you can do what you want. You've all got so much money to waste.

Simpson   Yes, well, I'm very sorry. But I told you at the beginning that I'd move as soon as I found a place of my own.

Landlady   When I was your age, I had more sense of responsibility. I would have gone to university myself if I'd had the chance. But in my day it was more difficult.

Simpson   I don't see what that's got to do with it.

Landlady   I'm sure you don't. But I've had to work hard all my life. If I'd had your opportunities, I would have got a good job. I'd have earned a lot of money and I'd have saved for my old age.

What should Simpson have told the landlady?
Would he have told her earlier if he had known?
What wouldn't she have done if she had known?
What else has he got to tell her?
What would she have done if she had had the chance?
What has she had to do all her life?
What would she have done if she had had his opportunities?
What would she have done if she had got a good job?

Ask me if
he should have told her earlier.
he'd have told her earlier if he'd known.
she'd have bought so much food if she'd known.
she'd have gone to university if she'd had the chance.
she'd have got a good job if she'd had his opportunities.

she'd have earned a lot of money if she'd had a good job.

Ask me
what he should have told the landlady.
what she'd have done if she'd had the chance.
what she'd have done if she'd had his opportunities.

19.5 Writing

Put the verbs in brackets into the correct form
1 She (buy) it if she had had the money.
2 He (take) you in his car if you had asked him.
3 There would have been trouble if I (be) there!
4 They would have taken you with them if you (ask) them.
5 If I had known he was a foreigner, I (speak) to him in French.
6 He would have come if he (be able to).
7 You would have done it if you (have to).
8 How long it (take) to get there if we had gone by bus?
9 What you (do) if he had caught you?
10 We (go) to the seaside yesterday if the weather had been fine.

Unit 20

20.1 Reading

You'd have had to get a work permit if you'd found a job

Jack	Mother.
Mrs Smith	Yes?
Jack	Could I go to France this summer for my holiday?
Mrs Smith	France? What on earth for? You went there for Easter.
Jack	But I want to stay for the whole of the summer this time.
Mrs Smith	It would cost far too much.
Jack	You said that last year. But I could have found a job.
Mrs Smith	If you had gone last year, you would have had to find a job first.

Jack	If I'd found a job. I'd have been able to make enough money to pay for my holiday.
Mrs Smith	If you had found a job, you'd have had to get a work permit.
Jack	That would have been easy.
Mrs Smith	Oh, would it? Anyway, even if you had got a work permit, you wouldn't have been able to stay long.
Jack	Why?
Mrs Smith	Because you'd have had to come back to school. That's why.
Jack	Well, all I know is, if I had stayed a couple of months I'd have been able to speak French fluently by now.
Mrs Smith	Here's our stop. This is where we get off.

What would Jack have had to do if he had gone to France last year?
What would he have been able to do if he had found a job?
If he had found a job what would he have had to get?
Would that have been easy?
Why wouldn't he have been able to stay long?
What does Jack think he'd have been able to do if he had stayed in France a couple of months?

20.2 Intonation

ˇMother. 'Could I 'go to ˋFrance this summer for my ˏholiday?

When you want to be persuasive or ask a particular favour, the voice falls and rises often on the same word.

Wendy is trying to persuade Hugh to buy her a coat. Everything she says, whether it is one word or a phrase, has the falling–rising tune.
Read the part of Wendy.

Wendy	Hugh.
Hugh	M'm?
Wendy	Put your book down a minute.
Hugh	Why?
Wendy	Listen.
Hugh	I'm listening.
Wendy	I saw a gorgeous coat today.
Hugh	Did you?
Wendy	Can I buy it?
Hugh	How much?

113

Wendy	Fifty pounds.
Hugh	What?
Wendy	That's not so much. Please.
Hugh	No.
Wendy	Hugh.
Hugh	No.
Wendy	You bought a suit last year.
Hugh	No, I said.
Wendy	All right. Hugh.
Hugh	What is it now?
Wendy	I bought a new hat today. Would you like to see it?

20.3 Oral practice

a)

An obligation you would have had if something had happened in the past

What did he say?
If you had gone to the States last year, would you have had to/get a visa?
/find a job?
/tell your wife?
/buy different clothes?
/borrow money?
/learn American?
/ask your parents' permission?
/book in advance?

What did he/she say?
Would you have had to make an appointment first if you'd gone to the doctor's?
you'd wanted to speak to your boss?
you'd had to see your bank manager?
you'd spoken to your husband before breakfast?

b)

An ability you would have had if something had happened in the past

What did he/she say?
If you'd had lessons, would you have been able to/drive a car?
/speak English fluently?
/play the piano?

What did   If you'd worked harder when you were young,
he/she say? would you have been able to/get a degree?
                                    /get a better job?
                                    /speak English well?

What did   If you'd wanted to, would you have been able to
he/she say? swim the Channel last summer?
                       stop smoking?
                       go to the States?
                       cook the dinner last night?

20.4   Listening comprehension

Hugh and Wendy relaxing in the garden

Wendy   I'm glad we didn't go for a drive today. It would have been too tiring.
Hugh   I would have enjoyed it.
Wendy   We'd have had to wait several hours in a traffic jam.
Hugh   If we'd gone, I'd have been able to have a swim.
Wendy   But the roads would have been so crowded. We wouldn't have been able to get out of London.
Hugh   Oh, it wouldn't have been as bad as that.
Wendy   Anyway, you didn't suggest going until half past eleven. If we had wanted to go to Brighton, we'd have had to leave early in the morning.
Hugh   I'd have been able to get there in an hour if I'd driven fast.
Wendy   You know I hate driving fast. And another thing – we'd have had to come back as soon as we had got there.
Hugh   Why?
Wendy   Because we'd never have got back home in all that traffic, of course.
Hugh   Oh well. If we had gone, it would probably have rained anyway. It always does.

Why is Wendy glad they didn't go for a drive?
Who would have enjoyed it?
How long would they have had to wait in a traffic jam?
What would Hugh have been able to do if they had gone?
Why wouldn't they have been able to get out of London?
When would they have had to leave if they had wanted to go to Brighton?

Would he have been able to get there in an hour if he had driven fast?
What would probably have happened if they had gone?

Ask me if
it would have been too tiring.
they'd have had to wait several hours in a traffic jam.
Hugh would have enjoyed it.
he'd have been able to swim if they had gone.
the roads would have been crowded.
they'd have been able to get out of London.
they'd have had to leave early if they'd wanted to go to Brighton.
he'd have been able to get there in an hour if he'd driven fast.

Ask me
how long they would have had to wait in a traffic jam.
what he'd have been able to do if they had gone.
when they would have had to leave if they'd wanted to go to Brighton.
why they would have had to come back as soon as they'd got there.

20.5 Writing

Put SHOULD HAVE/WOULD HAVE HAD TO/COULD HAVE *or*
WOULD HAVE BEEN ABLE TO *into the blank spaces, and change the verbs in brackets into the correct form*

1 I told you the theatre would be sold out. We . . . . . (book) our seats in advance.
2 He . . . . . (tell) me he was married.
3 Why didn't you tell me before? You . . . . . (do).
4 She . . . . . (go) to Birmingham yesterday, but she wasn't feeling well.
5 If he had gone by plane, he . . . . . pay more.
6 If we had bought that house, we . . . . . get a mortgage.
7 If he had wanted to go abroad, he . . . . . get a passport.
8 They . . . . . take their baby with them, if they had gone to the party.
9 If I had wanted to see him, I . . . . . make an appointment first.

10 I . . . . . (dance) all night.

11 He . . . . . (answer) all the questions, but they only asked him one.

12 You were at the station early. You not . . . . . (catch) an earlier train?

13 I . . . . . (go) yesterday, but he cancelled my appointment.

14 I . . . . . (go) to the dentist's yesterday, but I cancelled my appointment.

15 We . . . . . (ask) her husband as well, but he was busy.

16 I . . . . . buy a new car if I hadn't spent all my money.

17 They . . . . . pass the exam if they had worked harder.

18 If you had wanted to stay longer, you . . . . . get a work permit.

19 You . . . . . speak English well if you had stayed in England for two years.

20 I forgot I had an appointment with the dentist yesterday. I . . . . . (be) there at 10.15.

Unit 21

21.1 Reading

Just supposing

Peter   Would you like to go to the theatre tonight? There's a good
        play on at the Aldwych.
Alice   I wouldn't mind. But if we go, I'll have to get a babysitter.
Peter   That won't be difficult, will it?
Alice   I don't know. Betty would come if she could, but I think she's
        gone away for the weekend.
Peter   You could ring her up and find out, couldn't you?
Alice   Yes, I could. But we'd have to pay her more money if she

came. Last time she said we didn't pay her so much as the Jones's do next door.

Peter   Well, tell her that if we have to pay her more she'll have to get here on time. She should have been here at seven last Saturday and she didn't turn up till half past.

Alice   She said she couldn't get away from the office early.

Peter   She could have got away if she'd tried.

Alice   She'd have been here on time if her boss hadn't given her some extra work at the last minute.

Peter   She should pull herself together. She's too neurotic and bossy for me. She'll have a nervous breakdown if she isn't careful.

Alice   Anyway, I'll ask her to be here by seven. So if she gets here on time, we'll be able to catch the 7.20 train.

What will Alice have to do if they go to the theatre?
Who would come if she could?
What would they have to do if she came?
What will Betty have to do if they pay her more?
What time should she have been there last Saturday?
What excuse did Betty make for being late?
What will happen to Betty if she isn't careful?
What train will they be able to catch if Betty gets there by seven?

21.2 Intonation

Revision
Identify the following Intonation patterns and then read aloud. The numbers in brackets refer to the Units in which the pattern first appears.

George   Where shall we go for our honeymoon? (9)

Anne   Where? (10) Let's stay in London, shall we? (12)

George   In London? (10) Whatever for?

Anne   We'd save money that way. You'd like that, wouldn't you? (2)

George   I suppose so. (14) But I wish you wouldn't keep on implying that I'm mean. (15)

Anne   Well, you are, aren't you? (1)

George   No, I'm not. (6) I wouldn't take you out so often if I were mean. (19)

Anne   I pay. (17)

119

George	Oh, you do, do you? (18) Then don't forget to pay for the wedding, will you? (13) I want to be married in a Registry Office, but you don't. (4) You told me so yesterday.
Anne	Yes, I did, didn't I? (5) I wish I hadn't said that now. (11)
George	Why?
Anne	Because my parents can't afford it.
George	Anne. (20)
Anne	M'm?
George	Let's get married at once, shall we? (12) I'll pay for everything if we get married quietly. (19) I told you that ages ago.
Anne	So you did. (8) All right. But I'd book the time soon if I were you. (16) I might change my mind again.
George	So might I. (7)

21.3 Oral practice

What did
he say?

Will you go home by taxi if it's raining?
Would you go home by taxi if it were raining?
Would you have gone home by taxi last night if it had been raining?

Will you drive home if it's foggy?
Would you drive home if it were foggy?
Would you have driven home last night if it had been foggy?

Will you be home in five minutes if you take a taxi?
Would you be home in five minutes if you took a taxi?
Would you have been home in five minutes last night if you had taken a taxi?

Will you lend me some money if I ask you?
Would you lend me some money if I asked you?
Would you have lent me some money if I had asked you?

Will you help her if she asks you?
Would you help her if she asked you?
Would you have helped her if she had asked you?

Ask me if
I'll go home by taxi if it's raining.
I'd go home by taxi if it were raining.
I'd have gone home by taxi last night if it had been raining.

he'll lend me the money if I ask him.
he'd lend me the money if I asked him.
he'd have lent me the money if I'd asked him.

she'll help you if you ask her.
she'd help you if you asked her.
she'd have helped you if you had asked her.

21.4 Listening comprehension

Jean and Betty

Jean Have you heard the latest? George and Anne are getting married.

Betty Yes, I know. She rang me this morning.

Jean Just think. They would never have met if it hadn't been for me. I introduced them five years ago.

Betty Yes, but remember I introduced you to George first.

Jean So you did. So we're both responsible. How romantic.

Betty I don't think so. He wouldn't have asked her if she hadn't insisted. She's very bossy, you know.

Jean She knows what she wants, that's true. I remember when we were at school together she told me once that she would have liked to be Elizabeth I.

Betty Why?

Jean Because she could have sent her teachers to the Tower of London.

Betty She hasn't changed much, has she?

Jean You sound a little bitter.

Betty I am. You know I would have married George if he had asked me. I shall love him until I die.

Jean Poor Betty. Will you be going to the wedding?

Betty I'll go if they ask me. I'll have to, shan't I? I don't want them to think I'm jealous.

Jean I wonder what she'll wear.

Betty She'll have to wear something to cover those legs.

Jean Don't be wicked, Betty.

Betty Well, it's true. And you know, she never stops eating. She'll get very fat if she isn't careful.

Would George and Anne have met if it hadn't been for Jean?
Who introduced George to Jean?

According to Betty, would George have asked Anne if she hadn't insisted?

When Anne was at school, who would she have liked to be? Why?

Would Betty have married George if he had asked her?

How long will Betty love George?

Will she be going to George and Anne's wedding? Why?

What will Anne have to wear?

What will happen to Anne if she isn't careful? Why?

Ask me if

they would have met if it hadn't been for Jean.

Anne would have liked to be Elizabeth I.

Betty would have married him if he had asked her.

she'll be going to the wedding.

she'll go if they ask her.

Anne'll get fat if she isn't careful.

Ask me

who Anne would have liked to be.

what she could have done.

why Betty will have to go to the wedding.

what will happen if Anne doesn't stop eating.

21.5 Writing

Put the verbs in brackets into the correct form

1 Will he come to the party if we (ask) him?

2 Would he come to the party if we (ask) him?

3 Would he have come to the party if we (ask) him?

4 If I had known he was coming to the party, I (ask) his girl-friend too.

5 If you want her to come to the party, you (have to) ask her boy-friend too.

6 If you had wanted her to come, you (have to) ask her boy-friend too.

7 Do you think he would help me if I (ask) him?

8 I wouldn't marry you even if you (be) the last man in the world.

9 If you worked for that firm, they (expect) you to work overtime?

10 I'd like you to learn this by heart, if you (be able to).
11 He'd have liked me to help him if I (have) the time.
12 She'll get very fat if she not (be) careful.
13 If I had passed the First Certificate, I (be able to) start studying for the Proficiency.
14 If he goes to England, he (be able to) speak English.
15 If he went to Rome, he (be able to) see the Colosseum.
16 If he had gone to Greece, he (be able to) visit the Parthenon.
17 I (go) if I have to, but I don't really want to.
18 I'd go if I (have to), but I'd rather stay at home.
19 I'd have gone if I (have to), but luckily he couldn't remember my phone number, so he (be able to) tell me in time.
20 We'll be exhausted if we not (stop) soon.

Summary of Tenses

Unit 1   Present Continuous tense

Positive or *Affirmative*
subject + present of TO BE + present participle
I'm (I am) *teaching* English.
You're (you are) *learning* English.
He's (he is) *reading* a book.
She's (she is) *going* to the window.
It's (it is) *raining*.
We're (we are) *speaking* English.
You're (you are) *sitting down*.
They're (they are) *standing up*.

Negative
I'm not teaching French.
You aren't (you're not) *learning* Russian.
He isn't (he's not) *reading* a book.
She isn't (she's not) *going* to the window.
It isn't (it's not) *raining*.
We aren't (we're not) *speaking* Chinese.
You aren't (you're not) *sitting down*.
They aren't (they're not) *standing up*.

Interrogative
Are you learning French?
Yes, you are.   No, you're not.   No, you aren't.

Am I teaching English?
Yes, I am.   No, I'm not.

Is he reading a book?
Yes, he is.   No, he's not.   No, he isn't.

Is she going to the window?
Yes, she is.   No, she's not.   No, she isn't.

Is it raining?
Yes, it is.   No, it's not.   No, it isn't.

Are we speaking English?
Yes, we are.   No, we're not.   No, we aren't.

Are you sitting down?
Yes, we are.   No, we're not.   No, we aren't.

Are they standing up?
Yes, they are.   No, they're not.   No, they aren't.

The Present Continuous is used for an action that is happening at the moment of speaking. The action is happening *now*.

I'm taking her to the bus station.

It is also used for a continuous present action, but which is not necessarily happening at the moment of speaking.

I'm learning Russian at night school.

Unit 2   Present Continuous tense and the Future of Intention

The Future of Intention is formed by the present of
TO BE + GOING TO + infinitive

I'm going to ring up Anne and ask her to the pictures.

GOING TO expresses *the intention* now *to do* something in the future.

He's going to stay in Paris for a couple of days.
They're going to have lunch together.
He's not going to do it.
(He does not intend to do it.)

Note   When *am I going to see* you again?
(When do you intend to see me again?)
(See also Unit 4.)

The Present Continuous can also be used to express a future action. Usually with an adverb of time, it is used for a definitely arranged action in the future.

My boss *is arriving* the day after tomorrow.
My sister's *coming* to supper tonight.
He's *leaving* for Paris in the afternoon.

Compare   *I'm meeting* him this evening.
(Definitely arranged.)
I'm going to meet him this evening.
(That is my intention at the moment. The action will probably happen.)
See also section 1 of 'Reported Speech'.

125

Unit 3   a) Simple Present tense

Interrogative   DO/DOES + subject + infinitive without TO
Do I teach English every day?
Yes, you do.   No, you don't.

Do you come to school every day?
Yes, I do.   No, I don't.

Does he speak English well?
Yes, he does.   No, he doesn't.

Does she go abroad every year?
Yes, she does.   No, she doesn't.

Does it rain much in England?
Yes, it does.   No, it doesn't.

Do we study English twice a week?
Yes, we do.   No, we don't.

Do you have much fog in your country?
Yes, we do.   No, we don't.

Do they like learning English?
Yes, they do.   No, they don't.

Negative   subject + DON'T/DOESN'T + infinitive without TO
I don't teach English every day.
You don't come to school every morning.
He doesn't speak English well.
She doesn't go abroad every year.
It doesn't work.
We don't study English every evening.
You don't have fog in your country.
They don't like learning English.

Affirmative   subject + infinitive without TO
I go abroad every year.
You study English every week.
We work in an office.
You speak English very well.
They go to a football match every Saturday.

But the 3rd person singular (HE, SHE, IT) is followed by the
infinitive + s★
He works in an office.
She goes to England every year.
She washes the floor every day.

He watches television every night.
Time passes slowly.
He studies English every week.

★ If the infinitive ends in o, SH, CH, SS or X, add ES
go*es*, wish*es*, watch*es*, kiss*es*, fix*es*

If the infinitive ends in Y preceded by a consonant, change the
Y to I and add ES
study – stud*ies*
But if the Y is preceded by a vowel, add s as usual
pay – pay*s*

The Simple Present is used for habitual actions and permanent
truths.

Jack *goes* to school every morning.
The sun *shines* more often in Rome.

It can also be used for future actions taking place at an official
time, according to timetables etc.

The plane *leaves* London Airport at 14.32.
See also section 2 of 'Reported Speech'.

Note   Certain verbs are not usually used in the continuous form.
They take the Simple Present even when they express an
action that is happening at the moment of speaking.
Here are some of them.

be	Jack *is* at school at the moment.
believe	I *believe* it's a very good film.
cost	It *costs* a lot to go to Rome.
forget	I *forget* his exact words at the moment.
forgive	*Do you forgive* me for being so rude?
hate	She *hates* studying.
have	Anne *has* a television set. (have = possess)
but:	Anne *is having* a gin and tonic. (have = drink)
hear	*Do you hear* what I am saying?
know	I *know* I'm right.
like	She *likes* this television programme.
love	The Romans *love* life.
mean	I don't understand you. What *do you mean*?

remember	He *doesn't remember* what happened.
see	I *see* what you mean.
	but: *I'm seeing* him tomorrow. (see = meet)
seem	He *seems* very happy in his job.
smell	That soup *smells* good.
taste	It *tastes* good too.
think	I *think* you're very good at English. (opinion)
	but: *I'm thinking* of going abroad this summer.
understand	They *don't understand* what he's saying.
want	He *wants* to speak to you.

b) WHO, WHAT, WHICH, HOW MUCH? HOW MANY?
do not take DO/DOES (or any auxiliary) when they are
the subjects of a question

How many Germans DO *you* know?
How many Germans SPEAK English?

You is the subject of the first question, so DO is used to make
the interrogative.
How many Germans is the subject of the second question, so DO
is not used.

How much DOES *it* cost?	*How much rain* FALLS every winter?
How much DO *you* earn?	*How much of your salary* GOES in taxes?
Which book DO *you* want?	*Which student* SPEAKS the best English?
What DO *they* want?	*What* HAPPENS to gas when you light it? It burns.
Who DO *you* know here?	*Who* KNOWS you here?

Unit 4 Revision of Present Continuous, GOING TO, Simple Present

The Present Continuous expresses an action that is happening *now*.

Anne'*s smoking* a cigarette and *watching* television.

The Present Continuous can express an action that is happening
in the present, but not necessarily at this particular moment.

He'*s learning* Russian.

128

The Simple Present expresses an action that happens regularly.

I *go* to the cinema once a week.
She always *watches* TV at this time.

It is also used for permanent truths.

Florence *lies* on the River Arno.

A future action can be expressed:

1. with the Present Continuous
He *is flying* to Edinburgh tomorrow.
(Definite. Everything arranged. Adverb of time.)

2. with GOING TO + infinitive
He *is going to fly* to Edinburgh.
(At the moment he intends to fly. Not so definite as Present Continuous.)

Compare with:
He *is going* to Edinburgh by air.
(Definite. Everything arranged. He has bought his ticket.)

3. with the Simple Present
He's going to Edinburgh by air and the plane *leaves* at 15.00.
(Time stated by airline.)

The Prime Minister *returns* from Scotland tomorrow. (Official event.)

Remember some verbs do not take a continuous tense.

Note   Another use of GOING TO
I want to buy a car, and that's *going to take* every penny I've got.
(Speaker's certainty about a future action.)

I'm going home. It's *going to rain* in a minute.
(I think it will rain in a minute.)

Unit 5 a) Past tense of TO BE

Affirmative I WAS
You WERE
He/she/it/there WAS

We WERE
You WERE
They/there WERE

Negative I WASN'T (was not)
You WEREN'T (were not)
He/she/it/there WASN'T (was not)

We WEREN'T (were not)
You WEREN'T (were not)
They/there WEREN'T (were not)

Interrogative WAS I?
WERE you?
WAS he/she/it/there?

WERE we?
WERE you?
WERE they/there?

b) Past tense of TO HAVE

Affirmative subject + HAD
Betty *had* a headache last night.
He *had* the same car last year.

Negative subject + DIDN'T HAVE
They *didn't have* enough money to buy a house of their own.

Interrogative DID + subject + HAVE
Did you have the same car last year?
Yes, I did. No, I didn't.
Did he have a nervous breakdown?
Yes, he did. No, he didn't.

There are two other forms of negative and interrogative:
He *hadn't* the same car last year.
Had he the same car last year?
He *hadn't got* the same car last year.
Had he got the same car last year?

These forms can only be used when HAVE means *possess*.
When HAVE has another meaning, DID/DIDN'T must be used.

I *didn't have* breakfast this morning. ⎫ HADN'T or HAD HE GOT
Did he have a nervous breakdown? ⎬ cannot be used here.
DID/DIDN'T is always correct for interrogatives and negatives.

130

c) Past tense of TO HAVE TO

Affirmative subject + HAD TO + infinitive
I *had to go* straight to bed.
He *had to work* overtime three times a week.

HAD TO is the past of MUST. It always expresses an obligation in the past.

Negative subject + DIDN'T HAVE TO + infinitive
(Absence of obligation in the past.)
He *didn't have to work* any more.
I *didn't have to study* Latin at school.

Interrogative DID + subject + HAVE TO + infinitive
Did you have to get up early this morning?
Yes, I did. No, I didn't.

The forms HADN'T GOT TO/HAD YOU GOT TO? can be used in the negative and interrogative, but are not so frequent in spoken English.

d) Past tense of TO BE ABLE TO

Affirmative 1 subject + COULD + infinitive without TO
2 subject + WAS/WERE ABLE TO + infinitive

COULD and WAS/WERE ABLE TO express an ability to do something in the past.

He *could swim* when he was six.
He *was able to swim* when he was six.

But only WAS/WERE ABLE TO express an ability to do one particular action successfully in the past.

I *was able to answer* the last question.   (not COULD)
He *was able to get* here on time yesterday. (not COULD)

His wife *was able to find* a good job as an interpreter, because she *could speak* French and German fluently.

131

Interrogative 1 COULD + subject + infinitive without TO
2 WAS/WERE + subject + ABLE TO + infinitive

There is the same difference in meaning between these two forms in the interrogative as in the affirmative.

Could you swim when you were six?
Were you able to swim when you were six?
But
Were you able to answer the last question? (not COULD)
Was he able to get here on time yesterday? (not COULD)

Negative 1 subject + COULDN'T + infinitive without TO
2 subject + WASN'T/WEREN'T ABLE TO + infinitive

There is no difference in meaning between these two forms in the negative.

I *couldn't get away* from work early.
I *wasn't able to get away* from work early.
And
He *couldn't sleep.*
He *wasn't able to sleep.*

WAS/WERE ABLE TO express ability only, *never* permission.
COULD must be used for permission.

His father said he *could borrow* his car.

e) USED TO

USED TO expresses a regular action or habit in the past, which has now stopped.

Affirmative subject + USED TO + infinitive
Betty *used to take* three sleeping pills every night.
(But now she doesn't.)
You *used to go* to school by bus.
(When you were a child.)

Compare I *smoke* twenty cigarettes a day.
(I still do.)
I *used to smoke* twenty cigarettes a day.
(But now I don't.)

USED TO also describes something that existed in the past, but does not exist now.

There *used to be* a tobacconist's at the corner of this street. (But there isn't one there now.)

Negative   subject + DIDN'T USE TO + infinitive
subject + NEVER USED TO + infinitive

You *didn't use to go* to school by bus. } same
You *never used to go* to school by bus. } meaning

Interrogative   DID + subject + USE TO + infinitive
Did you use to live in London?
Yes, I did. No, I didn't.
Did there use to be a cinema there?
Yes, there did.
USED YOU TO?/I USEDN'T TO can also be used in the interrogative and negative, but are not so frequent in spoken English.

See also section 3 of 'Reported Speech'.

Unit 6   Past tense of Regular Verbs

Interrogative   DID + subject + infinitive without TO

Negative   subject + DIDN'T + infinitive without TO

Did you watch telly last night?
Yes, I did. No, I didn't.
My wife *didn't enjoy* it.

Affirmative   The past of regular verbs for all persons is formed by adding ED to the infinitive, or D if the infinitive ends in E.
to clean   I clean*ed* the windows yesterday.
to call   He call*ed* to see you this morning.
to dance   You danc*ed* with my wife for two hours last night.
to like   She lik*ed* dancing with you.

If the infinitive ends in Y and is preceded by a consonant, the Y is changed to IED.
to try   I tr*ied* to ring you.
to marry   She marr*ied* Jane's brother.

133

But: to play   Both teams play*ed* well. (preceded by a vowel)

> If the infinitive is one syllable ending in a consonant preceded
> by one vowel, the consonant is doubled before adding ED.
> to stop   I stop*ped* playing football years ago.
> to clap   The fans clap*ped* loudly during the match.

But: to greet   He greet*ed* me warmly. (2 vowels)

The Simple Past is used for an action completed at a particular
time in the past. The time is either expressed or understood.

We *watched* TV last night.
They *played* tennis yesterday.
He *asked* me a question (a minute ago).
I *enjoyed* the film very much (when I saw it).
See also sections 2, 3 and 10 of 'Reported Speech'.

Unit 7   Past tense of Irregular Verbs

See list of Irregular Verbs, page 155.

Unit 8   Past Continuous tense

Affirmative   subject + WAS/WERE + present participle
Negative   subject + WASN'T/WEREN'T + present participle
Interrogative   WAS/WERE + subject + present participle

Where *were you going* when I saw you in the street this
afternoon?
I *was going* home.

The Past Continuous expresses an action that continued for a
certain period in the past, often simultaneously with another
action.

WHILE George *was walking* along the street, he saw Anne.
We *were watching* television WHEN the phone rang.
She left the receiver off the hook, because she *was working* hard.

Compare   The old lady *got off* the bus and *fell*.
(First she got off the bus and then she fell.)

The old lady fell AS she *was getting off* the bus.
(She fell during the action of getting off the bus)

He *used to read* the paper while his wife *cooked* the supper.
(Habitual action in the past.)
He *was reading* the paper while his wife *cooked* (or, *was cooking*)
the supper.
(A continuous action in the past, but it happened only once.)

The Past Continuous is also used for an intended action in the
past, but which did not or is not going to happen.

I *was going to ask* you to the pictures.
(That was my intention.)
I *was only trying* to help.
(That was my intention, but obviously I am not helping you
at all.)

See also sections 1 and 4 of 'Reported Speech'.

Unit 9   **Present Perfect tense**

a)

Affirmative   subject + HAVE/HAS + past participle
Negative   subject + HAVEN'T/HASN'T + past participle
Interrogative   HAVE/HAS + subject + past participle
Note   All verbs in English take HAVE/HAS in composite tenses (except
in the passive).

I've (I have) just *arrived.*   *We've* (have) *been* there.
Have you been there?   *You've stopped* work.
He's (he has) *gone.*   *They've had* a good holiday.
She hasn't (she has not) *left* yet.
It's (it has) *cost* a lot of money.

The Present Perfect is used with the following adverbs to
express an action that did or did not take place in the recent
past.

JUST   YET   ALREADY   LATELY   RECENTLY

I *have* JUST *got back* from France.

She *has* ALREADY *left*.
They *haven't come* YET.
Have you seen any good films LATELY?

It is used with the expression: This is the first time/day . . .

This is the first time I've done this exercise.
This is the first day we've had any sun.

It is used after superlatives.

This is the *worst* spring we *have ever had*.
See also section 5 of 'Reported Speech'.

b) The difference between the Present Perfect and the Simple Past

The Simple Past expresses a past action that is finished. The time is stated or understood.

Pedro *wrote* to me *last week*.
When did you go to the hairdresser's?
I *went last Tuesday*.

The Present Perfect expresses a past action, but the time is not important. Only the action is important, and it is connected with *now*. The action may happen again in the future.

Pedro *has written* to me several times.
Where *have you been*?
I've been to the hairdresser's.

Compare *I've worked* hard this morning.
(Action in the past, but connected with *now*. It is still the the morning.)
I *worked* hard *this morning*.
(Action in the past, but said after lunch. No connection with *now*.)

How many cigarettes *have you smoked* today?
(Action in the past, but connected with *now*. Today is not finished.)

136

I *lived* in France for many years.
(The time is stated, the action is finished. Simple Past.)
I *have lived* in France, but now I live in Italy.
(The time is not stated and is not important. Only the action is important; the fact that I have lived in France. Present Perfect.)

Have you seen that film at the Odeon?
(The time is not stated, but the question refers to the past and includes the present. The film is still at the Odeon. Present Perfect.)

Did you see that film at the Odeon?
(The time is not stated, but the question refers only to the past. The film is no longer at the Odeon. Simple Past.)

The Present Perfect expresses an action which means *until now* or *in my life*. The exact time is not stated, but sometimes an adverb of frequency is used.

Have you EVER *been* to England?
They *have* NEVER *been* to England.
She *has* ALWAYS *done* her work well.
He *has* SELDOM *given* me any homework.

Have you been to the States?
(EVER is understood, *in your life – until now*.)

Unit 10   Present Perfect Continuous tense

Affirmative   subject + HAVE/HAS BEEN + present participle
Negative   subject + HAVEN'T/HASN'T BEEN + present participle
Interrogative   HAVE/HAS + subject + BEEN + present participle

The Present Perfect Continuous expresses an action that began in the past and is still continuing or has only just finished.

How long *have you been studying* English?
I *have been studying* English for a year.
(I began English a year ago; I have continued to study it until *now*, and I probably will continue in the future.)

He *has been working* since eight o'clock this morning.
(It is still the same day. He began working at eight o'clock this morning and has continued working until a short time ago. He has just finished working.)

See also section 6 of 'Reported Speech'.

SINCE expresses a specific time in the past.
It indicates the beginning of the action.

since Tuesday
since March
since 1973
since four o'clock
since last year
since he was twelve

FOR expresses a period of time.

for a week
for two hours
for the last six months
for many years

Unit 11   Past Perfect tense

a)

Affirmative	subject + HAD + past participle
Negative	subject + HADN'T + past participle
Interrogative	HAD + subject + past participle

The Past Perfect expresses an action in the past that happened before another action or before a certain time in the past.

After he *had gone*, I began to worry about him.
When I *had finished* lunch, I went out.
Had you seen the film before?

It is used with the expression: It was the first/second time/day that . . .

138

It was the first time he *had been* abroad.

See also Units 19 and 21.
See also sections 3, 5 and 7 of 'Reported Speech'.

Past Perfect Continuous tense

Affirmative subject + HAD BEEN + present participle
Negative subject + HADN'T BEEN + present participle
Interrogative HAD + subject + BEEN + present participle

The Past Perfect Continuous expresses an action that was continuing in the past before another action happened.

I was very tired because I *had been working* hard.
He *had been walking* for two hours before he arrived at the village.
See also sections 4, 6 and 7 of 'Reported Speech'.

b) FOR LONG/FOR A LONG TIME

Negative negative Present Perfect + FOR A LONG TIME
He *hasn't studied* English FOR A LONG TIME.
(And he is not studying it now.)

negative Present Perfect Continuous + FOR LONG
He *hasn't been studying* English FOR LONG.
(But he is still studying it.)

negative Past Perfect + FOR A LONG TIME
He *hadn't studied* English FOR A LONG TIME.

negative Past Perfect Continuous + FOR LONG
He *hadn't been studying* English FOR LONG.

Note Begin with the subject and the verb in English, *not* the time.

c)
The verbs BE and HAVE, and verbs like SEE, HEAR, KNOW do not usually take a continuous form with SINCE and FOR.

I *haven't been* TO England for a long time.
(I am not in England at the moment.)

I *haven't been* IN England for long.
(I am in England at the moment.)
He *hadn't been* in England for long before he got a job.
She *hasn't had* that dress for long.
I *haven't seen* you for a long time.
They talked for nearly three hours, because they *hadn't seen* each other for a long time.
I *haven't known* him for long.
I *haven't heard* that song since last summer.

Affirmative   He *has studied* English FOR A LONG TIME.   }   same
                He *has been studying* English FOR A LONG TIME. }   meaning

FOR LONG cannot be used in the affirmative.

Interrogative   *Has he been studying* English FOR LONG?   } same
                Has he been studying English FOR A LONG TIME? } meaning

                Hasn't he been studying English FOR LONG?   } same
                Hasn't he been studying English FOR A LONG TIME? } meaning

The Continuous form is always correct in the interrogative with FOR LONG/FOR A LONG TIME, except for verbs of perception and BE and HAVE.

Have you been here FOR LONG/FOR A LONG TIME?
Hasn't he known her FOR LONG/FOR A LONG TIME?

Unit 12   Future tense

Affirmative   subject + SHALL/WILL + infinitive without TO
                I'll (I shall) *be* thirty tomorrow.
                You'll (you will) *be* hungry by this evening.
                He'll (he will) *know* the answer.
                She'll (she will) *understand.*
                It'll (it will) *be* dark soon.
                We'll (we shall) *miss* the bus.
                You'll (you will) *be* late.
                They'll (they will) never *believe* you.

Negative   *I shan't* (shall not) *be* thirty tomorrow.
              You won't (will not) *be* hungry.

He won't (will not) *know* the answer.
It won't (will not) *be* dark soon.
We shan't (shall not) *miss* the bus.
You won't (will not) *be* late.
They won't (will not) *believe* you.

Interrogative   *Shall I see* you tomorrow?
Will you be hungry by this evening?
Will he wait for you afterwards?
Shall we go to the pictures?
Will you be late?
Will they lend you the money?

Students often confuse SHALL and WILL in the first person
singular and plural. Usually I/WE WILL means a strong desire
or intention to do something:
I will go.
We won't do it.
The difference between SHALL and WILL is not so important
today, as people in many regions of Britain use WILL for
all persons, or avoid the problem by saying I'LL/WE'LL instead
of I SHALL or I WILL.
In the interrogative, however, it is still better to use SHALL
for the first person singular and plural:
SHALL *I see* you tomorrow?
What SHALL *we* do?

Use of the
Future I   Unpremeditated intention: actions that the speaker has only just
decided to do or not do in the future.

I'll just *tell* the Sergeant where I'm going. *We won't* (or *we
shan't*) *do* this exercise to day.

Remember both the Present Continuous and the GOING TO
form express the future when the action has already been
arranged or when there is a premeditated intention to do
something in the future.

Compare   *I'll go* to the mountains tomorrow.
(I've just decided this minute.)
I'm going to the mountains tomorrow.
(I'm definitely going tomorrow. Everything is arranged.)

Offers

Will you have a cigarette?
Yes, please.
Shall I open the window?
No, thanks.

Requests

Will you shut the door, please?
Yes, of course. Certainly.

Suggestions

Shall we go to the cinema?
Yes, let's.

3   Future actions or events that are inevitable or habitual.

I'll be thirty tomorrow.
It'll be dark soon.

4   Speaker's opinion

I'm sure *he'll come* back soon.
I shan't be able to have a holiday this year.

5   Asking information about something that will or will not
happen in the future.

Whatever *shall I do*?
When *shall I see* you again?
Will he help you with your work?

6   The first type of conditional sentence (see Unit 21).

Future + IF + Present
He'll come back if he wants to.

A Future tense is *not* used after words like IF   WHEN   UNTIL
AS SOON AS

He'll come back IF we *ask* him.

He'll come WHEN he *is* ready.
I'll wait for you UNTIL you *arrive*.
I'll go AS SOON AS I've *finished*.

But the Future can be used after WHEN and IF when the speaker is not sure or has some doubt.

I'm not sure IF *I'll be able to go away* this year.
I doubt IF *I'll see* him.
I don't know WHEN *I'll see* him again.

The Future can also be used in the interrogative after WHEN.

WHEN *shall I see* you again?

See also sections 8 and 10 of 'Reported Speech'.

Unit 13 Future Continuous tense

Affirmative   subject + SHALL/WILL BE + present participle
I'll be (shall be) *seeing* you tomorrow.
He'll be (will be) *working* late tonight.

Interrogative   SHALL/WILL + subject + BE + present participle
Shall I be seeing you tomorrow?
Will he be working late tonight?

Negative   subject + SHAN'T/WON'T BE + present participle
I shan't be seeing you tomorrow.
He won't be working late tonight.

Use of Future Continuous 1   To substitute the GOING TO form in questions. This makes the question more polite.

How long *will you be staying*?
Shall I be seeing you tomorrow?

2   To express an action in the future that will start and continue for an indefinite period.

143

I'll be having dinner at that time.

I wonder what *I shall be doing* this time next year.

3 To express a future action (a) that will happen in the normal course of events; (b) depending on external circumstances.

a)

Compare   *We'll be serving* dinner in half an hour.

(As usual. That's the time we normally serve dinner.)

We're serving dinner in half an hour.

(Everything is organized and arranged.)

b)

He'll be staying in town till Saturday.

(Because he has got to work.)

He's staying in town till Saturday.

(He has arranged to stay, perhaps because he wants to.)

The difference between the Future Continuous and the Present Continuous to express a future action is very slight, and often either can be used. Remember, however, that the Present Continuous used for a future action always implies intention or pre-arrangement.

See also section 9 of 'Reported Speech'.

Unit 14   Revision of future actions

There are four main ways of expressing a future action:

1 Present Continuous *I'm seeing* him on Tuesday.
                              (Definitely arranged. Deliberate future action.)
          meaning: I've arranged to see him on Tuesday.

2 Future of Intention *I'm going to see* him on Tuesday.
                              (Premeditated action in the future.)
          meaning: I intend to see him on Tuesday.

3 Future   *I'll see* him on Tuesday.
                              (Unpremeditated intention. Sudden decision.)
          meaning: I've just decided to see him on Tuesday.

4 Future Continuous *I'll be seeing* him on Tuesday.
(Without deliberate intention. Often an action that usually happens in the future.)
meaning: I'll see him as usual on Tuesday.

Remember, however, that the Present Continuous, the Future and the Future Continuous have other uses as well (see Units 1, 12 and 13).

Unit 15   Present Conditional I

subject + WOULD + infinitive without TO
I'd like (would like) to go for a drive.
It'd be (would be) good for us to get some fresh air.

SHOULD is the grammatically correct form for the 1st person singular and plural, but in spoken English WOULD is being used more and more for all persons. This avoids confusion with the Present Conditional of HAVE TO – SHOULD (see Unit 17).

a)
The Present Conditional of both LIKE and WANT is WOULD LIKE.

Would you like to go to the States?
Yes, I would./No, I wouldn't.
Would you like a cup of tea?
Yes, please./No thanks.

b)
The Present Conditional of PREFER is often WOULD RATHER + infinitive without TO.

I would like to go to Switzerland for Christmas, but my wife *would rather go* to Egypt.
The negative is WOULD RATHER NOT + infinitive without TO
I'd rather not go to the cinema tonight, if you don't mind.

Unit 16   Present Conditional II

Present Conditional + IF + Past (see Unit 21)
I would go round the world IF I *won* the Pools.

After IF the Past of BE is WERE for all persons.
I'd think about it very carefully, IF I *were* you.

See also sections 8 and 10 of 'Reported Speech'.

Unit 17 Present Conditional III

The Present Conditional of TO HAVE TO is:

a) SHOULD/OUGHT TO + infinitive for all persons
For advice, suggestions

You should see a doctor.
She ought to see a doctor.

b) WOULD HAVE TO + infinitive

For obligation, the sensible thing to do
(WOULD HAVE TO is nearly always used with IF + Past)

I'd have to make an appointment first IF I *wanted* to see him this morning.
He would have to (he'd have to) learn English IF he *lived* in England.

HAD BETTER + infinitive without TO
HAD BETTER has a meaning between SHOULD and WOULD HAVE TO

You'd better (had better) call the doctor immediately.
(It would be better if you called the doctor immediately.)
He had better (he'd better) learn English if he's going to live in England.
(It would be better if he learnt English.)

Negative   *He'd better not speak* to me.
(This can be interpreted as a threat or a warning.)

Present Conditional of TO BE ABLE TO is:
c) COULD + infinitive without TO for all persons
For requests

146

Could you give me his phone number, please?
Could you speak to me in English, please?

For ability.

(If necessary) *he could speak* to them in English, French or German.
I'm not sure if *I could live* with someone like you.

d) WOULD BE ABLE TO + infinitive for all persons
For ability depending on IF something else happened

He'd be able to (would be able to) cover up my spots with something IF I *asked* him.
He would be able to (he'd be able to) speak English, IF he *studied* more.

For assumptions, suppositions.

He ought to/should speak English well by now.
He ought to/should be able to speak English well by now.
Henri should be here in a minute.

Unit 18   Past Conditional I

a)
The Past Conditional of TO HAVE TO is:
SHOULD HAVE + past participle for all persons

1 *He should have come* at eleven o'clock, but he didn't.
2 *We should have gone* to the musical instead of the play.

SHOULD HAVE expresses
1 an obligation or duty that was not done.
2 speaker's opinion about an action in the past.

Note   The pronunciation is SHOULD'VE not SHOULD HAVE.

An alternative is OUGHT TO HAVE + past participle for all persons
I ought to have gone to see him, but I didn't.
He ought to have rung me up last night, but he didn't.

147

This means the same as SHOULD HAVE, but is not used so much in spoken English.

b)

Negative   SHOULDN'T HAVE + past participle for all persons
You shouldn't have wasted all this time.
We shouldn't have been so late.

SHOULDN'T HAVE expresses the speaker's opinion about an action in the past.

Note   The pronunciation is SHOULDN'T'VE not SHOULDN'T HAVE.

An alternative is OUGHTN'T TO HAVE + past participle for all persons. This means the same as SHOULDN'T HAVE, but is not used so much in spoken English.

c)
The Past Conditional of TO BE ABLE TO is:
COULD HAVE + past participle for all persons

We could have got there on time, but we didn't.
He could have done so much to help my skin.

COULD HAVE expresses an ability to do something in the past, but the action was not done.

Note   The pronunciation is COULD'VE not COULD HAVE.

d)

Negative   COULDN'T HAVE + past participle for all persons
1   *I couldn't have sat* through that play without eating something first.
2   *You couldn't have been* that hungry.
3   He went to the cinema yesterday.
    He couldn't have gone, because he was ill.

COULDN'T HAVE expresses
1   an inability to do something in the past;
2   a negative supposition or
3   a contradiction of what someone has said about a past action.

Note   The pronunciation is COULDN'T'VE not COULDN'T HAVE.

148

Unit 19 Past Conditional II

The Past Conditional is formed with
subject + WOULD HAVE + past participle for all persons
followed by IF + Past Perfect

I would have gone to university IF I *had had* the chance.
(But I didn't have the chance.)

I would have told you earlier IF I *had known*.
(But I didn't know.)

See also Unit 21.
See also sections 10 and 11 of 'Reported Speech'.

Unit 20 Past Conditional III

a)
The Past Conditional of TO HAVE TO is also
WOULD HAVE HAD TO + infinitive for all persons.

Use this form when there would have been an obligation to do
something in the past IF a condition had been fulfilled.

You would have had to get a work permit IF you *had found* a job.
IF *we'd wanted* to go to Brighton, *we'd have had to leave* early.
Compare with SHOULD HAVE and OUGHT TO HAVE (Unit 18).

b)
The Past Conditional of TO BE ABLE TO is also
WOULD HAVE BEEN ABLE TO + infinitive for all persons

There is very little difference between WOULD HAVE BEEN
ABLE TO and COULD HAVE (see unit 18), as both forms
express an ability in the past. WOULD HAVE BEEN ABLE TO
is usually used with an IF clause giving a condition.

1 *I'd have been able to get* there IF *I'd driven* fast.
2 *We could have got* there on time (but we didn't).
COULD HAVE is also possible in 1 but WOULD HAVE BEEN ABLE
TO is not so possible in 2, because there is no IF.

Unit 21   The three Conditionals

Future + IF + Present
1 She *will marry* him IF he *asks* her.

Refers to a possible future action, which will happen if a condition is fulfilled in the future.

Present Conditional + IF + Past
2 She *would marry* him IF he *asked* her.

Refers to a future action which is possible, but the condition is less likely to be fulfilled.

Past Conditional + IF + Past Perfect
3 She *would have married* him IF he *had asked* her.

Refers to the past. The action cannot happen now because the condition cannot be fulfilled.

See also sections 10 and 11 of 'Reported Speech'.

Reported Speech

When the reporting verb is in the Present, Future or Present Perfect, there is no change from Direct to Indirect (Reported) Speech.

'I'm very happy.'
He *says* he's very happy.
He'*ll say* he's very happy.
He'*s just said* he's very happy.

But when the reporting verb is in the Past tense, the following changes usually take place.

I **Present Continuous** usually becomes **Past Continuous**
a) To express the future in the past.

'*I'm leaving* for Paris in the afternoon.'
George said *he was leaving* for Paris that afternoon.

But if the statement is reported immediately afterwards, the tense can remain unchanged.

'*I'm going away* for the weekend.'
What did he say?
He said (or, he says) *he's going away* for the weekend.

b) To express an action that is happening at the moment of speaking.

'*I'm trying* to get through the window.'
The thief said *he was trying* to get through the window.

2 **Simple Present** sometimes becomes the **Simple Past.**

'*I go* to the cinema once a week.'
Jim told Peter *he went* to the cinema once a week.

But when the Simple Present expresses an habitual action, the the tense can remain unchanged if the action is still habitual at the moment of speaking.

Jim told Peter *he goes* to the cinema once a week. (He still goes.)

(Jim told Peter *he went* to the cinema once a week can imply that he no longer goes to the cinema.)

The tense can also remain unchanged if reported immediately afterwards.

'My plane *leaves* at 17.10.'
What did he say?
He said (or, he says) his plane *leaves* at 17.10.
He said his plane *left* at 17.10. (Reported later.)

Permanent truths usually remain unchanged.

'Florence *lies* on the River Arno.'
The teacher explained to the class that Florence *lies* on the River Arno.

3 **Simple Past** usually becomes **Past Perfect**.

'*We went* to that new restaurant in the High Street.'
Bill said *they had gone* to that new restaurant in the High Street.

But the Simple Past remains unchanged
a) For habitual actions in the past.

'*I used to take* three sleeping pills every night.'
Betty told Jean *she used to take* three sleeping pills every night.

b) For an ability in the past.

'*She was able to find* a good job as an interpreter because *she could speak* French and German fluently.'
Jim explained that *she was able to find* a good job as an interpreter because *she could speak* French and German fluently.

c) For a fact.

'*I was born* in Norway.'

He said *he was born* in Norway.
'Shakespeare *wrote* Hamlet.'
The teacher told the class that Shakespeare *wrote* Hamlet.

d) For actions reported immediately afterwards.

'*I watched* TV last night.'
He said *he watched* TV last night.

4   **Past Continuous** sometimes becomes **Past Perfect Continuous.**

'*I was working* hard.'
Anne told George *she had been working* hard.

But usually the Past Continuous remains unchanged, especially with words like WHEN/WHILE/AS.

'I met Jack while *I was waiting* for you.'
Mrs Turnbull told her husband *she had met* Jack while *she was waiting* for him.

It remains unchanged for statements reported immediately afterwards.

'*I was working* for the same firm last year.'
(What did he say?)
He said *he was working* for the same firm last year.

5   **Present Perfect** usually becomes **Past Perfect.**

'*I've just got back* from France.'
Jack told Richard *he had just got back* from France.

Statements reported immediately afterwards need not change tense.

'*I've just arrived.*'
What did he say?
He said (or, he says) *he's just arrived.*

6   **Present Perfect Continuous** usually becomes **Past Perfect Continuous**.

'*I've been waiting* for nearly half an hour.'
Jean told Betty *she had been waiting* for nearly half an hour.

Statements reported immediately afterwards need not change tense.

'*I've been learning English* for two years.'
What did he say?
He said (or, he says) *he's been learning* English for two years.

7   **Past Perfect** and **Past Perfect Continuous** remain unchanged.

'*They had just come back* from Canada.'
Mrs Turnbull told Mrs Smith that *they had just come back* from Canada.

'*They hadn't been living* there for long before they moved to Scotland.
Mrs Turnbull said *they hadn't been living* there for long before they moved to Scotland.

8   **Future** becomes **Present Conditional.**

'*I'll give* you a ring about eight.'
Peter told Jim *he would give* him a ring about eight.

For statements reported immediately afterwards, the Future sounds unnatural in Reported Speech.

'*It'll be* dark soon.'
What did he say?
He said *it would be* dark soon.
NOT He said it will be dark soon.
BUT He *says* it will be dark soon.

9   **Future Continuous** becomes **Present Conditional Continuous** (not presented in this book).

'*I'll be staying* a couple of nights.'
Mr Simpson told the clerk *he would be staying* a couple of nights.

Like the Future, the Future Continuous changes for statements reported immediately.

'*I'll be going away* for the weekend.'
What did he say?
He said *he would be going away* for the weekend.
BUT He *says* he will be going away for the weekend.

10 **Present Conditional** remains unchanged.

'*I'd like* to do some gardening.'
Wendy told Hugh *she would like* to do some gardening.

'If I *won* the Pools *I'd go* round the world.'
Fred told Bert *he would go* round the world if he *won* the Pools.

Note   The Past tense after IF also remains unchanged.

In many languages the Present Conditional changes to the Past Conditional in Reported Speech. This is *not* the case in English.
   The Present Conditional always refers to the future, so it is logical that this tense cannot change to the Past Conditional in Reported Speech, because the Past Conditional always refers to the past in English.

   The only time the Present Conditional changes is when *the condition is no longer possible.*

'I'll marry him if he asks me.' ⎫
'I'd marry him if he asked me.' ⎬ Still possible
Betty told Jean *she would marry* George if he *asked* her.
(Still possible)

BUT: Betty told Jean *she would have married* George if he *had asked* her.
(No longer possible. George has married someone else, or he is dead)

11 **Past Conditional** remains unchanged.

'*She'd have been* here on time if her boss *hadn't given* her extra work.'
Alice told Peter that *Betty would have been* there on time if her boss *hadn't given* her extra work.

Irregular Verbs

Infinitive	Past tense	Past participle
be	was/were	been
bear	bore	borne, born
beat	beat	beaten
become	became	become
begin	began	begun
bend	bent	bent
bind	bound	bound
bite	bit	bitten
bleed	bled	bled
blow	blew	blown
break	broke	broken
bring	brought	brought
build	built	built
burst	burst	burst
buy	bought	bought
cast	cast	cast
catch	caught	caught
choose	chose	chosen
come	came	come
cost	cost	cost
creep	crept	crept
cut	cut	cut
dig	dug	dug
do	did	done
draw	drew	drawn
drink	drank	drunk
drive	drove	driven
eat	ate	eaten
fall	fell	fallen
feed	fed	fed
feel	felt	felt
fight	fought	fought
find	found	found
fly	flew	flown
forbid	forbade	forbidden
forget	forgot	forgotten
forgive	forgave	forgiven